Praise for Ashmi Pathela and *Anchoring the Light*

'This book is a force of remembering. It awakens something deep and ancient within – a knowing that we are already whole, already home. A transformative and gorgeous classic.'

ELLE MACPHERSON, FOUNDER OF WELLECO AND AUTHOR OF *ELLE*

'This is more than a book. It's a compass for seekers on a journey of remembering their core essence during these pivotal times. Ashmi's ability to channel heart-centered wisdom is unique and can be felt through every page. This is a template to becoming the "you" your soul came here to express.'

XAVIER DAGBA, TRANSFORMATIONAL COACH, SHADOW INTEGRATION GUIDE, AND AUTHOR OF *SCARS OF GOLD*

'*Anchoring the Light* is not a book – it's a portal into your own ascension journey. Ashmi channels a deep remembrance of who we are beneath the noise of this world. Her words are more than wisdom – they are frequency codes awakening our own soul knowing. This is a guide for New Earth leaders, empaths, and visionaries remembering why they came – and how to truly live from the light within. A map to light up the world the way we intended.'

CRYSTAL ALLEN, 'THE ENERGETIC ALCHEMIST'

'This book opens the door to a dimension bereft of past projections and lifted by the light of the heart. I felt grounded, yet weightless, as I was guided back to the heart's highest vibration embodied.'

JOEL CROSS, @ASOULCALLEDJOEL

'Pick up this book and immediately it will speak to your soul. As you connect with the truth of these words, you feel your heart begin to understand 'who you are' and 'why you are here'. It will touch the very essence of your being. A beautiful journey of self-discovery!'

BLOSSOM GOODCHILD, 'DIRECT VOICE' CHANNELER

'A beacon of light for those seeking profound wisdom, truth, and deep soul remembrance. More than a book, it's a divine blueprint and a powerful companion for those returning home to self.'

MELISSA HADFIELD, EXPANDING CONSCIOUSNESS

ANCHORING THE LIGHT

The New Earth Way of Living,
Creating and Becoming
All That You Are

ASHMI PATHELA

HAY HOUSE

Carlsbad, California • New York City
London • Sydney • New Delhi

Published in the United Kingdom by:
Hay House UK Ltd, 1st Floor, Crawford Corner
91–93 Baker Street, London W1U 6QQ
Tel: +44 (0)20 3927 7290; www.hayhouse.co.uk

Text © Ashmi Pathela, 2025
Cover painting by Bonnie Karuna Smith
Interior images: Freepik

The moral rights of the author have been asserted.

All rights reserved. No part of this book may be reproduced by any mechanical, photographic or electronic process, or in the form of a phonographic recording; nor may it be stored in a retrieval system, transmitted or otherwise be copied for public or private use, other than for 'fair use' as brief quotations embodied in articles and reviews, without prior written permission of the publisher.

The information given in this book should not be treated as a substitute for professional medical advice; always consult a medical practitioner. Any use of information in this book is at the reader's discretion and risk. Neither the author nor the publisher can be held responsible for any loss, claim or damage arising out of the use, or misuse, of the suggestions made, the failure to take medical advice or for any material on third-party websites.

A catalogue record for this book is available from the British Library.

Tradepaper ISBN: 978-1-83782-289-8
E-book ISBN: 978-1-83782-291-1
Audiobook ISBN: 978-1-83782-290-4

10 9 8 7 6 5 4 3 2 1

This product uses responsibly sourced papers, including recycled materials and materials from other controlled sources. For more information, see www.hayhouse.co.uk

The authorized representative in the EU for product safety and compliance is Penguin Random House Ireland, Morrison Chambers, 32 Nassau Street, Dublin D02 YH68, Ireland. https://eu-contact.penguin.ie

Printed and bound by CPI Group (UK) Ltd, Croydon CR0 4YY

For the light-warriors, the dreamers, and the softest of hearts...

For you, for humanity, for all those who have journeyed into the depths of their darkness to find their way to their light.

Contents

Introduction:	*A Story*	ix
Chapter 1:	You Are Here for a Reason	1
Chapter 2:	Remembering Who You Are	9
Chapter 3:	A Global Shift in Consciousness	21
Chapter 4:	A New Navigating System	45
Chapter 5:	Journeying into Becoming Everything	69
Chapter 6:	The Dance of Light and Shadow	83
Chapter 7:	Walking Between Worlds	101
Chapter 8:	Transcending Your Programming	123
Chapter 9:	Dissolving Separation	141
Chapter 10:	Embodying Your Light	163
Chapter 11:	Creating as the Quantum Field	189
Chapter 12:	A New Earth	213
Onward		229
Thank You		237
About the Author		239

Introduction: A Story

In the beginning, there was Oneness. And Oneness, bored of simply *being* for millennia, wanted to experience itself. It wanted to experience all that it could be.

Oneness grew curious about what else it could be. It yearned to experience all the facets of itself, all the faces it could be.

And so, it shattered itself into millions of pieces, like a giant kaleidoscope. From one soul, infinite souls were born – each colorful shard an expression of the One.

The souls spread across the galaxies to experience life through their own lenses. They wanted to experience the limitlessness of existence, so they took the forms of all kinds of beings imaginable – some more physical, some more light – inhabiting all the dimensions of creation. They created new worlds, new realms of existence. Many had children. Most chose to express themselves as love, while some chose to express themselves as hate, greed, and the abuse of power.

Oneness saw no right or wrong, simply the beauty of expansion. It relished the endless possibilities… the ecstasy of growth, change, and variety.

These expressions of Oneness knew who they were and where they came from. They had so much fun experiencing themselves, creating whatever they could imagine, while also remembering the Oneness that they had come from, the light that they were.

One day, Oneness wondered, *What will happen if I forget who I am?*

And the moment the thought was formed, the experiment was born.

Earth became the home of that experiment. It was a jewel of a planet, beloved by all the beings in the galaxies, vibrant with stunning landscapes and billions of expressions of life.

It was the perfect place for Oneness's questions to be answered:

~ What happens when a soul forgets its source?
~ What becomes of creation when it has forgotten it is also the creator?
~ Who will souls choose to be when they don't remember who they are?

Curiosity set the experiment in motion, birthing a new type of being: humans.

In ancient times, many of the humans had memories of who they truly were. But century upon century, this connection faded until it became a whisper, a restless missing of something they could no longer name. In the early years of childhood, most forgot who they were and where they had come from. Some remembered, but their memories were often written off as imagination and, in time, faded away.

Many lived life after life forgetting the highest truth, the Oneness from which they had come. Many sleepwalked through life – numb, lost, and afraid. No matter how hard they tried, they felt unfulfilled. No matter what they achieved, it never felt enough. Something was missing.

Introduction: A Story

They had difficult childhoods, even more painful adulthoods. They were plunged into the depths and extremes of emotion, and it was unbearable at times. But in spite of it all... they loved. They kept going. They held the flame of hope in their hearts. They dreamed of a better day.

They kept coming back to the one thing that made them feel connected, that made them think, *There must be more to life than this...* And this was love.

Their love cast a web of light across the entire planet. Love – their first instinct, their human nature, their soul's essence.

They could hear the voice of love from deep within, whispering, 'Remember who you are. Remember why you're here. Remember where you come from.' But, try as they might, they could not remember. They grasped and yearned, crying out, 'What is it that I'm missing?'

And so, Oneness spoke directly to the heart of humanity. Quietly but clearly, addressing anyone who would listen:

'As I speak to you, remember... you are me, and I am you. You came from the stars. You are love. You are infinite. You are one. We are one.

Keep going, keep going. You are remembering who you are. In this lifetime, you will remember.

You are the brave ones, the bravest of the brave. You are the bearers of the light, the ones illuminating the path for all to come. You are on Earth to experience all that you are and all that you wish to be.'

And slowly, they remembered. They came home to the love inside their hearts. They remembered who they were and why they were here.

And they were free.

CHAPTER 1

You Are Here for a Reason

'Who am I?' Throughout your life, you have been asking yourself this question in so many ways, yearning for the answer. Whether you realize it or not, you have been asking the world: 'Am I good enough?'

You have likely searched high and low for validation of your worth – in your family, friendships, relationships, work… and in your own heart. Perhaps at the core of these questions there has been an unconscious yearning to feel that connection with your spirit, your soul, the Oneness you come from – your true self. In this life, you have experienced what it's like to feel utterly alone, disconnected from your soul – and you have been yearning for home.

You have been seeking your truth in your inner depths because, as a soul, you know there is so much more to you than you know. There is so much more to life than this. Throughout your life, you have suffered so much pain, journeying into the darkest depths of your being: utter despair, frustration, and loneliness. You have felt it all, not only in this lifetime, but across millions of lifetimes and dimensions… infinite timelines of experience.

If you are here now, you have known the greatest pain possible, the heaviest density that exists, the weight of the world on your shoulders. And at times, you have not known if you could keep going.

You have felt it all. You have walked through the fiery belly of the shadow. And this is why, despite everything you have endured, you still have hope… and this is why your heart can be so bright, pure, and full of love.

This is why you are here now, awakening at this time on Earth, realizing there is so much more. You are seeking the answer to who you truly are and why you are here – here among an entire world of humans who have forgotten who they are, denied themselves their heart, lost touch with the infinite magic of their soul.

You are the bravest of the brave, the most loving of souls… and still, you got swept up in the harrowing trials of being a human on Earth. Of course you did. There was no greater challenge than to be here.

And at the same time, the experience has been a gift, because to wake up from the illusion of fear and separation is the most breathtaking of feats and the greatest of joys… And here you are now, insisting on shattering every illusion.

> *Here you are, insisting on remembering – and becoming – all that you know yourself to be.*

And you will succeed. You will remember who you are. You will live from that place of wholeness and love. It will ripple out into your life, and nothing will ever be the same…

This is a journey close to my heart, because I've been there. Throughout my life, I've asked myself over and over again:

- 'Who am I?'
- 'What am I here to do?'
- 'Am I good enough?'

I spent my life chasing external milestones to prove to myself that I was 'making progress,' that I was 'good enough.' As a child, I felt the most seen when I achieved, and so I pushed myself to be the best in all my endeavors – from school lessons to piano recitals, from art to sports… I was always the hardest on myself, sprinting even faster whenever I fell short, and I became an over-achiever in everything in life.

I did the same with personal development, constantly pushing myself to improve so I could finally feel like I'd arrived.

And all along, there was an exhausted little girl in me wanting to know that it was safe to be myself, that I was good enough just as I was.

Ignoring that girl, I forged ahead. In my early career, I worked for fast-paced technology companies in Silicon Valley. I was in the belly of it all, from working at Facebook (now Meta) in its early days of becoming a social media giant to being there at the birth of new start-ups and witnessing the exponential growth of software companies.

Year after year, I took on more responsibilities, until one day I became the chief-of-staff to the CEO, his right-hand woman – the only woman in a room full of executives. In fact, I began to act on behalf of the CEO, as he was dealing with health issues and was unable to be present in the office most days.

I lived and breathed this life, working from 7 a.m. to sometimes 10 p.m. or midnight, even 2 a.m. I ate meals at my desk or on the go between meetings, rushing to keep up with never-ending deadlines. Weekends and holidays didn't matter. This life became my everything.

The executives told me, 'You're a machine!' as if that was something to be proud of. And to be honest, I was proud of it. I thought I'd found my purpose. I felt seen and respected.

The CEO said, grinning, 'I wonder what it would take to break you?'

I didn't know, but at the same time, I was waking up every day with heart palpitations, my body in fight-or-flight mode, running on overdrive.

Gradually, slowly, then all at once – I broke.

How? There was the time I had a full-blown anxiety attack that left me zapped like a zombie on the couch for hours, the time I broke down crying on the street corner outside the office, the time we had to fire over 40 employees because the company was imploding – and everything we had worked so hard for evaporated at once.

And during those long months that felt like rock bottom, I started asking myself:

~ 'What is it that I truly want?'
~ 'What would happiness really look like for me?'
~ 'How do I want to define success?'

Little did I know that this was my soul nudging me to come back to myself, come back to my heart, come back to the place I had strayed so far away from for so long.

I was utterly exhausted, mentally and physically, but a couple evenings a week, whenever I finished work early enough, I started going to a late-night café in my neighborhood. I wanted to carve out some time for myself, to journal and reflect. I wrote about my dreams, my fears, the longings of my soul. The words didn't flow smoothly every time, but I could feel a tiny flame igniting in my heart. It felt energizing to take back some time for myself, when it felt like virtually every other hour of the day was for others – my boss, my team, my stress. Those quiet hours in that café gave me fleeting glimpses of what it felt like to reconnect with myself, and I wanted more.

The answers started to come:

~ 'Leave this job.'

~ 'Listen to your heart.'

~ 'Take time to come back to yourself.'

Finally, I listened. Within the space of three months, I left my job and turned my back on that Silicon Valley career pinnacle that I'd been working so hard to reach. I started freelancing so that I could work remotely and booked a spot in a coworking retreat with people who were also searching for more.

Though I was terrified, my heart felt strangely buoyant, filled with hope. I knew this was the most radical leap I had ever taken, and it would change the trajectory of my life. I was thrilled by the grand promise of the unknown path ahead. The most magical journey was available to me, if I chose to rise and meet it.

One evening, on a rooftop under the stars, I spoke this intention to the universe: 'Show me the power of my heart, and I will teach the world.'

Little did I know the heart has a way, and it was already guiding me... and it would take me to places beyond my wildest dreams.

Thanks to my flexible work schedule, I created spaciousness away from the noise for the first time in my life – time and space to meditate, journal, walk in nature, and reflect. I began to hear the voice of my soul – quiet at first, but always there. It began to shine through the voice of my fears.

And the more I stepped away from what society told me I should do and be, the more I began to see myself, and life, through fresh eyes. I began to feel what it was like to follow my heart, trust my inner voice – and walk in union with my soul.

It has been the most magical journey of my life, and I hope to share this magic with you – the power of living true to your soul, knowing all that you are, and feeling the endless love that exists within you, the love that blesses everything in your life as you walk *as* your soul.

We are living in an unprecedented time on Earth. More people than ever before are yearning for a new way of being, one guided by love and possibility, not fear and limitation, in which we can feel free, alive, and at peace.

We have felt the suffocation, the deep pain of being disconnected from ourselves, for long enough. Now, the nudges of our souls are getting stronger, and many of us are wondering, *Is it safe to follow my heart? Is it safe to be myself?* Many of us are determined to find the answers, even if it means the death of everything we thought we knew.

This book was written for this monumental time. It is an activation for the soul, for *you*, to help you expand your consciousness beyond limitation and courageously walk into a new way of being. In these pages, you'll find channeled wisdom, gentle encouragement, and empowering shifts – not just about awakening, but about *embodying* the light that you are, anchoring it on this beautiful planet at this incredible moment of ascension.

Humanity is going to places we've never been before, and everything is changing, from external systems to our fundamental ways of thinking, living, and creating. This book provides a new navigating system for life and a breathtaking vision of a New Earth beyond limitation.

The following pages will share codes for consciously anchoring higher frequencies, dissolving separation, and becoming the quantum field. They will also provide techniques for clearing lifetimes of fear and programming from your cellular structure. You'll learn how to trust yourself, open up to your inner guidance, and live as your highest self now… so you can unlock the beautiful new ways of being, creating, and thriving that will become available to you.

This will change life as you know it. Ultimately, you will create a life – and world – of your wildest dreams, from the frequency of knowing *you are all there is.*

This may seem impossible – irrational even. But this is a book channeled from the heart, not written from the mind. These words aren't just for your mental understanding; they offer a frequency activation, a transmission, of how it feels to embody the light of your soul, so that you can unlock this within yourself. As you read, let go of the need to make sense of everything logically, because *beyond* the human mind is where you will find your knowing, your gifts, your infinite light…

> *Take a deep breath, and allow your heart*
> *to savor and receive these words.*

Trust that your soul has called you to this book for a reason: to activate your own remembering.

Deep down, you already know everything there is to know. It is just time for you to remember. Above all, to remember who you are.

CHAPTER 2

Remembering Who You Are

You are the highest frequency of love, embodied in physical form. And you are so much more than this body, this lifetime, this name. The magnitude of what you are doing now – awakening, expanding your consciousness, ascending to places you have never been before – is enormous.

It takes immense courage to choose this path, to come to Earth and forget all that you are, to descend into the density of your emotions, your mind, your fears… and take on the tremendous task of finding your way, crawling blindly into the light, to remember who you are.

You have felt the entire spectrum of polarity on a planet where you've lost the lifeline of knowing who you are and where you come from as a soul.

And yet, here you are. You are the light. You have always been the light.

No matter how lost you have felt, your soul has always been cheering you on. And the entire multiverse is mirroring back to you the love that you are. Once you open your heart to receive it, you will feel it in the depths of your being. You will know it in your bones.

Shifting Dimensions

When you feel the light that you are, when you let it flood into every cell of your being, you will realize it isn't coming from outside of you. It is coming from within your own heart, your DNA, your cellular structure. You are anchoring and embodying the light of Source and cycling it out into the world. This is a natural part of what you do and who you are.

The highest frequencies of light are coming from *you*, as you activate them within yourself and send them out into the world. Once you remember that you are the light, once you step into this knowing, there will be no fear, no doubt. No illusion of separation. Still, you will observe polarity. You might witness challenges coming up in your reality, but the fears and emotions that used to take you away from yourself will flow through you like water. You will be fully present, seeing the world and your life through the eyes of love.

You will be the witness, the observer, of your reality. And at the same time, you will *know* you are the creator of it all. And this is the frequency that will change everything.

First and foremost, it will change the frequency you operate from. Everything is energy, vibrating at a certain frequency, including matter, sound, and color. The denser it is, the slower its vibration. Your frequency fluctuates based on your thoughts, beliefs, fears, and emotions, both conscious and subconscious. As you clear the density in your being and open your heart, your frequency rises, which shifts the dimension that you experience.

A dimension is a frequency through which you experience life. For centuries, most of humanity has been experiencing life from the third dimension. This is not a place, it is a way of being and thinking. It holds the programming of fear and lack, limitation and scarcity, survival and competition, ego and control.

Every day, you are constantly shifting dimensions, constantly fluctuating in frequency, until you can hold the higher frequency in your body long enough to anchor yourself into a more expansive dimension. You may not notice anything has changed, because everything looks the same, but there will be a lightness in your thoughts, emotions, and interactions.

Then your outer world will shift to match the frequency you hold, and beautiful new realities will materialize. You will be in awe of the lightness of your steps, the magic in the mundane, the vividness of the world coming alive around you, the amount of love that flows out of your heart, the amount of love you allow yourself to receive from the world around you.

When you remember who you are, and live from that place, all the timelines and realities of struggle, lack, and fear will melt away in the light of who you are. You will walk in full faith, feeling your inner spark of divinity flowing through you and out into your entire life, and into the world.

The frequency of knowing who you are will ripple out into everything you do, create, and experience. This frequency will bless your creations, the people in your life, and everything you love. It is a new way of interacting with your physical reality – and you came here to play in these higher frequencies, to experience the deliciousness of this physical reality. You wanted to feel your power to create, to love, to experience, to express yourself as a soul in *this* dimension. And the next, and the next.

As you shift dimensions, you will be able to see what is no longer serving your highest good and collapse those realities, simply with your awareness. They are old programs, memories, and patterns that are no longer true to who you are and who you are becoming.

When you see them, you can tell yourself:

- ~ 'I no longer choose to feed this fear.'
- ~ 'I no longer choose to react.'
- ~ 'I no longer choose to make myself small.'

And, over and over again: 'I no longer choose to be unconscious.'

On this journey, you first practice becoming conscious – aware of yourself, connected to your heart, aligned with your soul – as often as you can remember, until you naturally hold this state of awareness at all times. Then you won't have to try to be conscious, you will simply exist as consciousness, embodying the light of your soul.

You will remember that this is your reality and everything is happening for you. And this will allow you to trust and let go of the need to control. This in turn will open you up to the flow of divinity that you are, allowing the universe to create through you, *as* you, by you.

This frequency of *being* will ripple out into everything, creating a life that will feel absolutely magical to your old self. Here, you experience 'miracles.' But they aren't miracles, they are expressions of the natural order of the universe.

When you accept the magic of who you are,
you allow it to be reflected back to you
from your reality.

The highest timeline will materialize in the most beautiful ways, beyond anything you think you can try to control yourself – because it is orchestrated by your highest self, by Source, *by the light that you are.*

Beyond Where You Have Ever Been

This is an invitation to trust that you are already opening up to this brand-new way of being and living. And this is how the New Earth comes to life... through your heart. The more you allow it, see it, and accept it as your truth, the more it animates around you. You will see it come to life in every moment, every interaction, everything that you are.

It is called 'the New Earth' because it has not yet been lived by any incarnation. It is the future of life on Earth, the world you are creating. It is called 'New' because it is the new you, for you are not only remembering who you are as a soul, you are creating all that you wish to experience yourself to be. You are going to places your consciousness has never gone before – and all the old rules must be thrown out the window. They cannot come with you.

You are called 'the new human,' for this leap in consciousness is beyond any leap ever taken in the history of the cosmos. You are creating and re-creating yourself in the image of who you truly are. It is magical to get to experience what it's like to be a soul, an eternal being of light, in an embodied physical experience.

And so, you are new. In every moment. This is why it is essential to be present and come back to your heart. Everything is available to you now. Your mind says, 'This is crazy!' but your soul says, 'This is exciting!'

This is what you came here for – you came here to expand your idea of who you are, to see yourself as the light, in the context of the greatest polarity and shadow to ever exist on this physical Earth plane.

You came here to claim the light that you are and illuminate the world around you. As you walk this path, you'll go through many deaths and rebirths, to the point where you'll be unrecognizable to your old self. And at the same time, you'll feel more yourself than you've ever felt. You'll feel connected to the core of who you are, your essence, your childhood innocence – the pure light of your divine inner child.

You'll also embody the wisdom of your highest self, the most expansive frequency of your soul. You'll integrate the mastery of the lifetimes in which you experienced yourself as a priestess, a sage, a galactic being, and more. These are all human labels, and in a way, they don't matter. Even in those lifetimes, you experienced separation, seeking more outside of yourself, and now you're going much further than you've ever been, even in the lifetimes when you were the most connected to spirit.

You will unify all the aspects of your infinite soul. And you'll get to choose which aspects to keep and which to lovingly discard. For example, you'll remember the lifetimes that you spent in density and struggle, even the ones where you hurt others and did things you're not proud of. But you'll see it all through the eyes of love and realize you had to experience it all.

Every life, every experience, has served a purpose, and the lessons are being integrated in you now. You had to experience all the aspects of consciousness, the polarity of shadow and light, in order to be here now… to be who you are now. It has all been for your highest expansion… because it has brought you to this moment.

We will explore more of the interplay of shadow and light in Chapter 6, but for now, come back to who you are.

The Light of Your Soul

What is the soul? It is who you are. It is the spark of light, of divinity, of Source, that you are.

Many humans think they *have* a soul. But they *are* a soul. You *have* a human body in this physical experience, but you *are* a soul.

You may relate to your soul as your own spark of light. And this is true from one perspective, but from the highest perspective, all souls are one. They are one consciousness. You can think of it as a frequency or an energy of unconditional love.

Your soul is an expression of this energy, the energy of Source. At the root of it all, your soul *is* Source. In other words, *you* are Source.

Most humans feel safer playing in more limited expressions like 'You come from Source' or 'You are a spark of the divine.' From one perspective, this is true. But zoom out further, and you will see that there is no separation, no 'end' to your soul that separates you from other souls. It is all connected – you are all of it:

You are Source.

You are consciousness experiencing itself. You are a brilliant shard of the swirling kaleidoscope of life – and at the same time, you are the entire kaleidoscope. You are the observer and the artist. You are the music, the dancer, the choreographer. All of it is you.

These words allow you to tune in to this concept, but the full knowing of it is vast, infinite. The all-encompassing love that you truly are is much bigger than the greatest unconditional love you have felt, and once you glimpse it and know it as the truth of who you are, it will change everything.

∞

You are waking up to who you are. Everything that does not align with your true essence is crumbling. And so, even the outdated systems are collapsing. As an old soul, lightworker, starseed (whatever you choose to call yourself), you have come into this life with the deep knowing that a better way is possible. Though your human self may have forgotten, your soul knows that you came here to create a new world. It is in your DNA.

All the challenges, disappointments, and heartaches of your life have nudged you to remember this core part of yourself. In this life and many others, you have been pushed into a box. And your frustration has been compounded because your soul knows that you came here for the opposite: a life of freedom and peace, one that is possible for the entire world as humanity awakens.

Humanity *is* awakening, and you are paving the way for a whole new experience of life. We are all one and connected, awakening together, but it takes those who are courageous enough to dream a bigger dream for the world and ask themselves, 'What if?' to set it all in motion.

You are doing that now. As you shift, the consciousness of the planet is shifting. With every fear you face, you clear the way for yourself and the collective. Every time you love yourself more, your love ripples through your entire lineage.

Imagine souls as threads of a divine, infinite tapestry. Those who resonate as wayshowers, lightworkers, and starseeds – you who are reading this now – are lighting up with brilliant golden light. And the millions more beautiful souls out there who do not know they are lightworkers are also shining their light.

The golden light ripples out from these threads, spreading through the tapestry. And, wave by wave, thread by thread, the entire tapestry becomes shimmering light… changing the fabric of reality.

This is one way to visualize the awakening of humanity, the ascension of the planet – and it is happening, thread by thread, wave by wave.

You are already shining that light, because you are tuning in to the higher frequencies that are now available, opening your mind and heart to new dimensions of truth and love that you perhaps rejected, or could not see before. You are freeing yourself, saying, 'No more,' to what no longer resonates, following your heart, sharing your love with those around you in your unique way. You are ascending yourself – and so, the collective is ascending as one.

As you awaken and focus on your ascension, your union with your soul, this light ripples out into the world, into all of humanity, across all dimensions.

And so, when you shift yourself,
you shift the entire world.

The more you connect with your heart, the more you will feel the energy of your soul come through. You will feel your connection to all that you are.

In this lifetime, you are learning to trust the guidance of your soul – its wisdom, gifts, and voice – rather than the voice of your mind. You are learning to trust your knowing, rather than your fears, the disempowering narratives that you tell yourself, and the societal programming and conditioning that tell you, 'This is how it is.' You are learning to trust the limitless perspective of your soul rather than the limits that have been placed on your reality that you've internalized as fact.

Death, for example, is just a shedding of the physical body. If you see it through physical eyes, it will feel like an ending. However, to the soul, there is no real death. Your consciousness lives on.

Moreover, at the end of every lifetime, through death, you return to the full remembering of who you are as a soul, as Source, as Oneness. You awaken to the realization that you never actually left Source while you were having the experience of life on Earth.

So far, you have had to experience physical death to return to that realization of who you truly are – to know it not just as a concept, but as your total experience. But this time on Earth is special, because you will be able to keep your physical body with you as you come into the remembrance of who you are as a soul.

There have been rare individuals throughout your history who have ascended while in their physical body. Others have glimpsed the Oneness that they are during a near-death experience, or had a fleeting moment of nirvana in meditation or their dream-state. But this is the first time on Earth that you will ascend into the full knowing of your oneness with Source without having to die first. This is the first lifetime in all of eternity in which you will remember who you are while keeping your body with you.

Your body holds the memories of all lifetimes in which you had to die to 'return' to Source and remember who you truly were. In many lifetimes, it was a traumatic, scary, or lonely death. So, a part of your consciousness will worry: 'Am I going to die? Do I have to die again to get back to that place?' Be gentle with yourself, as this is a fear held in your cellular memory. Now you can experience the connection you have been yearning for from lifetime to lifetime…

You chose to come into this life for this moment… for this experience on Earth – and to create what is next.

Here is a letter that was channeled for you. As you read it, you are invited to imagine it is a message from your soul.

A LETTER FROM YOUR SOUL

Dear sweet soul,

I know that you're both scared and excited, and it feels like an entire world of the unknown is stretching in front of you. You are so brave for choosing to follow your soul when you don't know where it's leading. You are courageous for walking away from everything you've ever known to give the life your heart yearns for a chance.

You have no idea where this path will lead, but I promise you, everything is blooming for you. In just a few short months, you'll see evidence of this. In less than a year, you'll pinch yourself because you can't believe how fast your dreams are coming true… and in less than five years, you'll be standing in the middle of your wildest dreams, with tears of joy streaming down your face. All of this and more is pouring in for you, and this is just the beginning.

This decision to choose your soul is the biggest decision of your life. It will change the trajectory of everything and open doors you never knew existed. It is the portal to your heart's deepest desires and a life beyond what you believe is possible. Ultimately, it is the portal to yourself – becoming who you truly are, falling in love with yourself, and stepping into the full radiance of your light.

And it is worth it. It is worth everything. Yes, you'll meet your fears and walk through the inferno of your inner dragons. Yes, you'll journey blindly into the darkest crevices of your being. Yes, there will be days when you want to quit and hide. But you are strong enough to continue. You are here for a reason.

I love you.

Your soul

CHAPTER 3

A Global Shift in Consciousness

Your journey of awakening to all that you truly are isn't happening by accident. It is part of a greater shift that is taking place all over the world.

Something is happening on Earth on a scale that has never happened before. You might notice it in the quiet rumblings, the stirrings, of your heart. You might notice it in the chaos seemingly erupting in all corners of the Earth. You might notice it in the suffocation of your soul, in the yearning for life to feel easier, lighter, freer. Humanity is going through an unprecedented shift in consciousness.

As part of this process, old paradigms are being overturned, systems are collapsing, trusted authorities are being exposed. The dark underbelly of consciousness that has been hidden for centuries is coming up to the surface to be seen... and the entire world is being cleansed in order to make way for the new.

Individually, billions are facing their fears, making life-changing decisions, leaving jobs or relationships, changing careers and dreams – questioning their beliefs, no longer willing to put up with old ways that aren't working anymore.

> *The whispers of your soul are getting louder,*
> *telling you to let go of your fears and*
> *follow the call of your heart.*

It's becoming more obvious that something's off about the world. Look at the staggering amount of depression, anxiety, and debt… the astronomical gap between rich and poor, the never-ending cycle of working to get by, the increasingly busy and distracted lifestyle that is tearing families apart. In this 'modern' world, why are our life-expectancy and fertility rates decreasing? Why is there still so much hunger and war? This is not how it was meant to be. Part of you knows this, because you – your soul – simultaneously exists in other lifetimes, realms, and dimensions that feel so much freer than life on Earth.

It may even seem like the world is getting darker and more divided, especially if you watch the news, but the darkness has been here for centuries. It only appears to be intensifying now because it's coming to the surface, waking the masses from their deep slumber. It is being seen by more eyes than ever before, felt by more hearts that are calling for change.

Most people have not been aware of the extent of the corruption that exists on Earth, how it has woven itself like a web throughout almost every system and institution in every corner of the world. Now you are witnessing the exposure of the corruption and manipulation that have been ingrained in almost every major institution and system – from politics to medicine, banking, education, the media, and so much more.

While there are countless beautiful souls who work in these industries, these systems have been manipulated over decades by the few at the top who lust for power, control, and money. They believe a disconnected population is easiest to control. You have been told these systems exist to serve humanity, but they have been distorted to keep you divided, sick, in debt, brainwashed, and in fear – complacent enough, tired and distracted enough, not to question the narrative.

It would take entire books to go into all of this, and much of it will be revealed in the coming years… But this book isn't about blaming the system. It is about empowering yourself to awaken and realize that everything that has been happening in the world is for your highest expansion.

Awakening to what's been going on in the world can feel as if the rug is being pulled from underneath your feet, your world is turning upside down – and you don't know what to believe anymore. But know this: the world is going through a monumental rebirth.

Like a bright spotlight, the light that is flooding the entire world is illuminating all of the shadows. Everything that was hidden underground is coming to the surface to be seen.

This is happening collectively and also individually – your suppressed fears, emotions, traumas, pains, and the beliefs that don't serve you are all coming up because they cannot be ignored anymore.

The polarity in the world is a reflection of the division, lack, and judgment humans hold within. So, you are being pushed, more than ever before, to look within, let go of what is not fulfilling you, and dream of a new way. As heavy as it can feel, this process is bringing more light to this planet than ever before, illuminating all the shadows, overturning everything that is no longer serving us. It is birthing dreams of peace, love, and freedom for all.

What is happening is not just a monumental shift in consciousness. It is a full-body ascension, which means you are upgrading your physical body as you anchor the highest frequencies of all that you are, merging all aspects of your soul, and unifying all dimensions within as one. This shift is not just an energetic experience. It is an intensely physical, deeply embodied experience. It is changing your DNA as well as your cellular and molecular structure. It is changing your species. And this has never been done before.

This time on Earth has been prophesied for millennia. From ancient civilizations to modern mystics, many have spoken about how everything will change as we enter the Age of Aquarius, a new 25,920-year cosmic cycle. This has been prophesized to be a time of total transformation and renewal. Others have explained this shift by saying higher frequencies in the form of solar flares are hitting the planet and interdimensional beings (other aspects of you, of Source) are assisting the Earth in this transition.

This can bring comfort. And from one perspective and dimension of experience, it is true. But know that from the highest perspective, this ascension isn't the result of anything external. You are one with it all, and there is nothing separate from you, nothing outside of you. And so, you are the one creating it all.

You are the one ascending yourself, because you as a soul chose to experience this.

∞

Throughout this book, I will share the story of what happened when I left Silicon Valley and started paving my own path – the paralyzing doubts I faced and how everything began to bloom. But first, I will share an experience that melted away every shred of doubt I carried about the ascension and where my life, and this world, was headed.

When I first heard about the ascension during the months of soul-searching after I left Silicon Valley, it made my heart soar with hope, but my mind spin with doubt. I thought it sounded too wild to be true, but at the same time I felt an inexplicable resonance. It was as if my soul was jumping up and down, saying, 'Yes! You are starting to remember why you came here.'

A few years later, I had a magical experience that gave me a taste of what it felt like to exist in a higher dimension. I was sitting on the couch with my partner, Joel (who is now my husband), in a reality that was very different from the one I'd left in California just a few years earlier. We were living in Western Australia, and I had just started writing my first book. I'd met Joel at a café in Bali exactly a year after I'd left my full-time job in Silicon Valley. My soul had recognized him the moment I saw him, and there was a palpable magic between us that drew us together. After almost a year of a long-distance relationship and many tender visits, I moved across the world to be with him.

It was a normal evening. We were chatting animatedly on the couch about consciousness and awakening, as we often did, when all of a sudden the energy palpably shifted. I felt buoyant and calm at the same time, my mind suddenly quiet, my body totally relaxed. But it was more than that – it felt like a different frequency, a new dimension.

'Do you feel that?' I asked.

'Yeah, you feel that too?' Joel replied. 'What just happened?'

I was blown away that we were both feeling the same thing at the same time (and no, there were no drugs, alcohol, or other substances involved). It was like I had melted into pure presence, without any effort. There was no rush. No need to do anything or be anywhere. I could breathe deeply and fully, with ease, and I felt truly alive for the first time in my life.

I remember feeling amazed by the lack of stress and tension in my forehead. All of my worries had evaporated completely. But it wasn't like a euphoric high – I felt clear and more grounded in myself.

This is the energy of the New Earth. This is how it feels to exist in a higher frequency, in another dimension, and it is coming in waves as the consciousness on the planet shifts.

And most of all, Joel and I felt our undeniable connection to our souls, each other, and Source in a way we had never felt it before. We felt the presence of Source everywhere, in everything, and especially within us. We had no doubt that the divine was supporting us.

Both of us felt this way for 10 days, with the same level of unshakable calm and buoyancy sustaining us the entire time. We only needed about five hours of sleep at night, but we woke up absolutely energized and clear every morning. We went about our days as if in a lucid dream, marveling at synchronicities happening left and right, feeling completely supported and surrendered… And it truly felt like everything was happening *for* us, *through* us.

From the outside, those 10 days looked absolutely ordinary. We were working, running errands, cooking dinner, washing the dishes… But everything was different because of how we felt. While driving, it felt like the lights turned green for us just as we arrived at the intersection.

Even when a car dangerously pulled out in front of us, forcing Joel to slam on the brakes, instead of getting rocked off-center, we were totally unruffled. We felt completely safe and guided, overcome by the unshakable feeling that we were exactly where we were divinely meant to be, in every moment, big and small – and nothing was out of place, including the few seconds we had to slam on the brakes.

Held by the energy of that week, we felt inspired to start creating videos together about the awakening journey, so we went to the electronics store to buy a camera. The kindest shop clerk helped us choose the right camera and dug up an amazing deal for us. At the register, the camera, tripod, and all the equipment we needed ended up being exactly the same amount as the value of the credit card points we had available to use for the purchase – down to the dollar. Again, we felt the hand of the divine in every experience.

All of these things, alone, may sound coincidental, but they kept happening, one after another, and we felt like little kids marveling at the universe for the first time. The world came alive with blessings and synchronicities because we were embodying the frequency of seeing everything as happening for us.

Even breathing felt luxurious, as if every breath was nourishing my body. While washing the dishes, I found myself utterly present without having to try, simply enjoying the feel of the water running over my hands. And all I could think was, *This frequency is everything. This is all that matters. This is where we are heading. I wish everyone in the world could feel this. It would change everything.*

And it will, because this is the ascension.

Those 10 days were a gift from my soul, a taste of what was to come. But our bodies could not yet sustain this frequency permanently. We knew we had to go deep, to clear the density in our being and work through our doubts and fears.

And this is how you anchor the light – by clearing your density and creating more space to hold it in your cells.

Becoming the Quantum Field

You are everything, and so you exist everywhere. Your soul is experiencing itself in infinite lifetimes, dimensions, and realities all at the same time. And yet, this fragment of your soul is only aware of itself in this lifetime, because this is where your consciousness is focused.

Even though sometimes you may wish to be anywhere but here – even though in your darkest hours you may have wished to leave this planet, leave this life, because it was too hard… there is nowhere else your soul would rather be. This moment, this life, this reality, is what you came here for.

In this lifetime, your consciousness is expanding much further than ever before – and it will become aware of all that you are, beyond this fragment of your soul, beyond this life.

This ascension process dissolves all separation, so that you are no longer just the self – you become the entire quantum field.

The quantum field is everything that exists, everything that has ever existed, and everything that could possibly exist. It is the infinite potential of consciousness. From the highest perspective, just as you are already ascended, you are already the entire quantum field. But in your individualized lifetimes in these realms where you experience density, you exist in the illusion of separation. Your body and energetic field are part of the quantum field, but you perceive yourself as separate from it and everything around you. You have not yet ascended your body to become one with the quantum field and hold this expanded embodiment as you walk through life.

In spiritual circles, many have viewed this ascension process as a journey into the fifth dimension and beyond – the higher dimensions where freedom, peace, and limitlessness become your default frequency and experience. But it is a misconception that this ascension is solely about rising into the higher dimensions. It happens within your body, because nothing is outside of you. Instead of ascending into the higher dimensions of existence, you are unifying all the dimensions within you and collapsing the separation between them.

It has been helpful for humans to picture the dimensions as outside of them. This is one way to look at it, but in truth the dimensions are not a ladder outside of you to climb. Visualizing the higher dimensions as above you or outside of you only adds to the illusion of separation; it is more effective to visualize the dimensions as within you, encompassing one another like the layers of an onion.

The dimensions all exist within you. And they are not actually separate from one another; you only experience separation between them because your mind creates the separation, and humanity has been perpetuating this illusion for so long.

On this ascension journey, you are expanding to access and anchor higher dimensions, and ultimately merging all the dimensions within your being again. Once you do this, you will be able to access reality from any dimension you choose and move between the dimensions with ease. You use your frequency to tune in to any dimension, and you can even navigate between multiple dimensions simultaneously.

As you unify all the dimensions within, you dissolve the layers of separation and come to know yourself as Source.

*You realize that while you are human,
you are so much more.*

Expanding into all that you are generates an immense amount of light, radiating from within you. This shift in consciousness, combined with your physical and energetic expansion, activates your lightbody. Your lightbody is your energetic body, your true essence embodied in physical form. And it is activated by this ascension process: everything you're doing to illuminate your shadows and alchemize density into light.

Your physical body is going through enormous changes every day, as your shift in consciousness literally restructures your DNA, activates your cells, and integrates the higher frequencies into your vessel. This allows you to receive the full functionality of your DNA, activating the dormant strands currently labeled by scientists as 'junk,' which begins the process of transforming every particle of your body to hold more light, shifting your body from carbon-based to crystalline.

This process is physically intense, and there are hundreds of ways you may notice your body adjusting to the upgrades, which is unique to everyone – from headaches in your forehead (third eye) to high-pitched ringing in your ears, extreme lethargy requiring you to rest and sleep, changes in appetite and diet, vivid or lucid dreams, dizziness, and more. You may see these as uncomfortable 'symptoms,' but they are actually signs your body is being activated and is undergoing the transition process.

Over time, your body will feel stronger, younger, and lighter – because it is no longer carrying the density of your limitations, stress, and lack-based programming. You will unlock new abilities to regenerate your body, opening your mind and heart to the idea that you can actually live much longer than you have been told. And you will become a new human, with your DNA functioning completely differently from the way it has been. It will be a brand-new experience of what it's like to be the light in human form.

Ultimately, your ascension – or, more accurately, your unification – leads to you becoming the quantum field while maintaining your physical form. In this state, you will be both you in your body and all there is; you will be able to hold the multidimensional awareness of yourself in this form as well as the infinite facets of your soul. It will feel seamless to travel between the different aspects of yourself, explore the realms of the multiverse, and choose where you want to focus your awareness. While this is impossibly vast for the human mind to hold, by this point you will have expanded far beyond the mind and be operating from the higher mind, the higher heart, the infinite consciousness that you are.

When you become the quantum field, you will know, without a shadow of a doubt, that you are everything. This knowing will flip everything inside out, upside down (or right side up)… It will change existence as you know it.

You are already walking the path toward becoming the quantum field, and this is why you may feel like over the years you have been pushed beyond your limits to question everything, let go of your old identities, and face the fears and emotions you have been suppressing.

Becoming the quantum field requires you to let go of your sense of self. To truly know yourself as everything, you must dissolve your concept of self.

Self as separate.

Self as small.

Self as just a human.

This can feel like the ultimate death, but you aren't really dying. You aren't really losing yourself. You are letting go of your small sense of self to merge with all that you truly are – the love that you are, the consciousness that permeates all.

Over the years, you may have found comfort in being yourself, feeling appreciation for who you are… the way you live, think, feel… for your personality and how you navigate life. It can feel like you are being asked to let go of this as you expand into the Oneness of your soul beyond this human existence. But you aren't losing your individual spirit; you are bringing it with you, as you walk into the embodiment of all that you are.

You are just shedding your limitations – everything that holds you in separation: the fears, limiting beliefs, traumas, and old programming. These are energies you have agreed to play in until now. Once they are shed, what will remain is truth – the truth of who you are. And this will be the most liberating experience, freeing you from the density, allowing you to bring the wisdom and gifts from this lifetime and all others into every moment.

In countless lives, you have been misunderstood, rejected, or even killed for being your true self. But this time, the world is ready for you. It is time to shine your light.

Embracing Your Divinity

For many lifetimes, you have been the black sheep of your family. You've resisted being squeezed into a box or told what to do, refusing to be defined by the world. And it has not been easy. You've been wondering, 'What am I supposed to be doing?' because your soul came here for a reason, and you have long forgotten its name.

You have journeyed into the depths of your loneliness, thinking no one can understand you or fully see you for who you are. Sometimes, it felt like you were screaming into the void, with no one to answer, no one to hold you.

This awakening journey can feel even lonelier, because it turns your entire world upside down. It makes you seek answers the world cannot give you and open up to truths that feel absolutely crazy to admit. It has been a lonely and restless search, because the answers aren't out there. They cannot be found outside of you.

It may feel like you're going on this journey alone, but this is only because you are in the early waves of an entire species that is going through this monumental ascension – and most are not yet aware of it. But wave after wave, eyes are opening, hearts are opening… millions are awakening, day after day, in pockets around the world. You may not be able to see it or feel it yet, but there will come a day when you don't doubt it anymore… when you will see it with your very eyes: an entire world, awakening, ascending – and it will be the greatest sight you see.

Until that time, it is normal to fear becoming more alone on this journey, less relatable to your friends and family. As you rise, you will wonder if you are leaving people behind, if this path will get more isolating as you go…

You may ask yourself, 'If I connect more with my divinity, will I lose my humanity?' It's true that you will naturally shed aspects of your humanity that do not serve you – your fears, your lack, many of your beliefs, and your conditioned ways of being. This can feel like the death of the old you, as already mentioned, and the death of life as you've known it. But remember, it is not just your humanity that makes you relatable. It is your heart.

> *Your heart is where your divinity meets your humanity. The love in your heart is the purest, most beautiful truth of who you are.*

So, this journey isn't about discarding your humanity for your divinity, but about bringing your humanity with you, the most remarkable *heart* of humanity, and unifying it with the divine that you are.

It is safe to ascend, dear soul. You are not leaving anyone behind. You are not leaving yourself behind. You may be afraid to shine and be seen for who you are, because you don't want to be judged. But if your light triggers others, it is only because your energy makes them see what they have been hiding from and feel what they have been ignoring within. Often, your light can be like a bright flashlight, illuminating for others the shadows they hold within. And at the same time, it offers a bright reflection, allowing those who are open to see the beauty and light in themselves. This is simply what happens when light enters a room.

So, it is only through ascending yourself that you lift up others. It is *only* through this that the entire world can shift like a reflection in the mirror. In response to you. It is safe to open the doors to divinity. Wait until you see who is on the other side…

It is you. It has always been you! It is safe to open the floodgates of light. On the other side is more of your own soul. There is nothing to be afraid of. You are just allowing the final separation to dissolve – the idea that you are separate from others. The more you let go of the idea that 'they' don't get it, or 'they're' not like you, or you're better or lesser than 'them' (whatever is coming up for you in your shadow), the more you will shift into the experience that you are one, rather than separate.

This is how you achieve the collective ascension of your entire species: letting go of the idea that 'they' are separate from you. You cannot leave anyone behind, because you cannot leave yourself behind. You are just waiting for all of you to come to the remembrance that you are one.

Across lifetimes you believed you had to be alone to get to where you wanted to be, that you were better or lesser than others, that you could never be accepted for who you were. Now you are healing those experiences, forgiving those who persecuted you. You are realizing that no one was actually judging, rejecting, or persecuting you. It was always you judging yourself, rejecting yourself, persecuting yourself… creating the experience of separation because you believed you were not whole, that something must be wrong with you.

It takes the monumental undoing of all lifetimes, all that you have known, to clear the separation and start seeing everything as one. But for the entire planet, the entire species to ascend, you must let go of all beliefs held in separation. Humanity has never ascended as a collective species before, in any existence or dimension on Earth, precisely because separation still existed within your consciousness.

In the past, individuals have ascended. You call them ascended masters or enlightened ones, rare visionaries, and yogis who have attained union with their body, mind, and spirit to become the Oneness that they are, embodied in physical form. Some have gone on to other dimensions, and others have returned to Earth, to this dimension, as their ascended selves.

But they had to do it alone. They still held the idea that they were different, that they had to be an example, or that they had to walk the journey alone. They still experienced judgment, and even hatred, from those who did not understand them. The consciousness of humanity wasn't ready for them, and so this was their experience.

But now the world is opening up, the world is changing, and humanity is more open to the frequency of unity consciousness than ever before. You are becoming more open to the idea that experiences of divinity aren't just for the special few. You are worthy enough to have them, just as you are.

These are momentous times. Never before has an entire species gone through a full-body ascension, from a place of complete amnesia to the total remembrance and unification with who they are. Not on this Earth. Not in this multiverse.

And in addition to your species, your entire planet is ascending – the earth, the trees, the animals, every grain of sand… all rising in frequency, mirroring the shift you are creating within. For the first time, you are collectively creating the entire ascension of your planet.

At a soul level, you don't want to experience this journey as your individual ascension, while the rest of the world remains asleep. You are choosing to experience this as a collective ascension into all that you are, an ascension beyond all ascensions – all aspects of your infinite soul awakening and ascending across time and space.

This lifetime is your proudest creation as a soul, precisely because it has been so difficult. It is easy to create when you know you are a powerful creator. It is hard to create when you have forgotten who you are. No other creation in the multiverse can compare to the triumph of what you are doing now, birthing the ascension of your species after eons of lifetimes spent in complete amnesia. This feat is a testament to your consciousness, rising as one.

You have created this entire reality so you can experience the creation of yourself, the remembering of all that you are. And through that experience, you are giving your soul a new depth, a new love for yourself, a new appreciation of existence. This is how you keep expanding upon your idea of who you truly are – and all that you can be.

This will create a brand-new reality. This will create a brand-new way of being. This will create a brand New Earth. And existence will forever be changed.

Do not wait for the world to awaken. First, awaken all of yourself.

Do not wait for the world to ascend. First, ascend all of yourself.

> *Do not wait for others to remember they are the light. Remember you are the light, and all that you are is light.*

There will come a time when you will feel it in your bones…

You will see the entire world awakening and rising as one. This will be the sign that your inner unification is complete. This will be your confirmation that it's happening within you and outside of you.

You will be in awe of what you have done, alongside your brothers and sisters on this Earth. You will be filled with so much pride and joy... Tears will flow freely, and the sight of your world, flooded with light, bursting with love, will take your breath away.

Never underestimate the power of holding this vision, sharing it, and speaking of it. This is what ripples out into the world and brings forward the highest timelines for humanity... This is what creates waves of change and shifts everything.

VISIONS FOR THE NEW EARTH

It is sometime in the future, and the children and grandchildren are gathered around us by an open fire. They are listening intently, eyes wide, jaws dropping open, as we tell them our story... the story of humanity, of the years when it looked like everything was falling apart.

We tell them about how we came together, how we stood for love, for freedom, for them. And how the world changed.

We tell them about how the world used to be back then. How we were unknowingly enslaved in fear and limitation... the deep yearning to be free that sparked a global awakening.

And they cannot believe their ears. Because all they know now is pure peace. Freedom. And joy, for all beings.

Because of us.

If this vision feels far away, remember that this ascension is inevitable, because you have already chosen it. The momentum of all the experiences of your life that have led you to this moment, here and now, is already taking you on the highest path to a place beyond your wildest dreams. It is inevitable, and at the same time, your awareness and intention allow you to support your journey, assisting in your expansion instead of resisting it.

Here is the paradox. From one perspective, you are already ascended. There is a reality, a timeline, where you already exist in your ascended state; you are now simply experiencing the ascension that has already occurred in that timeline. It is already done. There is no time, and everything is happening all at once: all lifetimes, realities, and timelines. It is hard for humans to fully understand this, but quantum physicists have touched on it.

In this dense physical realm, time feels real. It exists as a construct, and everything is slowed down here. And even though your ascension has already happened in the highest dimensions – is happening in this moment now, which is all there is – you have chosen to experience it up close in this life, in slow motion, for your soul. It is an absolute gift for the soul to be able to experience it moment by moment, slowly enough to drink it all in, take part in its unfolding, and experience the emotions of it. Everything you learn and create here leaves an imprint on your soul, rippling out to touch all of consciousness forevermore.

You are walking into an inevitable convergence – the union of all that you are, your current self meeting your future self. You can trust your path, knowing your ascension is already done. Let go of thinking you're behind, you need to do more, or you're not listening to your soul enough. Let go of being so hard on yourself, because that's coming from the mind of judgment and doubt.

From another perspective, you are actively participating in your ascension in every moment on this Earth plane – and everything you experience here matters. All of it serves to expand your consciousness. Your awareness, intention, and frequency direct what you experience.

Every moment is exactly where you need to be – but the key is to get out of your own way and trust the journey.

You did not come here for the end result.
You came here for the journey, with all of its
wild twists and turns, ups and downs.

Here is one way to visualize it. Imagine you're driving a car on the path of life. And your whole life, you've been gripping the steering wheel tightly, concentrating mightily, because you don't want to miss any turns. You don't have a map, and you're second-guessing which way to go… rushing, wanting to get there before the others, and at the same time, afraid of crashing. And you're exhausted.

You don't know this, but if you were to relax your grip on the metaphorical steering wheel, you would realize that your highest self, your soul, your universe was helping you steer the car. You aren't going to crash, because you've always been guided.

Then you realize this is a magical car, and this road, this journey, even the car – all of it is made for you. There's no way you can take a wrong turn, because all roads lead to your highest knowing of your soul and all that you are. And in every moment, you're exactly where you're meant to be.

This doesn't mean you don't get to choose your journey. You are your highest self, and you are always choosing. And this doesn't mean you can stop caring and participating. It means you can let go of your fears and allow yourself to enjoy the ride.

The more you let go, the more exciting it gets. The more you let go, the more easeful it gets. The more you let go, the more you start appreciating the vibrant scenery passing by… You roll down the windows, turn up the music, and feel the wind in your hair. You allow yourself to enjoy this moment, because you know that you're going to get there, exactly when you need to. And right here is all that matters.

A New Earth Emerging

The world today can be visualized as a planet of light splitting from a planet in shadow. The shadow is visible, but it is an echo of the past. The true frequency of the Earth now, held in place by nature, is so much higher than you think. This is the direction humanity is heading in – exponentially releasing the shadow to anchor more light than ever before.

The shackles of the past are melting away, though your mind may trick itself into thinking it is still chained to the old patterns. But your consciousness is catching up with the true present moment, the frequency that the Earth is holding now – a much higher frequency than ever before. Your consciousness is playing catch-up to the reality that is available to you now.

When you go into nature, you'll feel that the Earth has shifted. There's so much more peace and love that you can tune in to and access within your own heart.

Leaping into the new when the entire world is still insisting on the old ways, stuck in the shadow, and living from fear, lack, and overthinking, requires a complete dissolving of all the ways of being you have known. But if you hold on to your outdated belief systems, fears, and pain, you won't be able to tune in to the higher dimensions that are here now.

It can feel utterly crazy. This is because the New Earth way is a complete inversion of the old. It can feel irrational, opposite to what the world says you should be and do, opposite to everything that has been the norm.

> *You are shifting from the mind into the heart, from fear to faith, from limitation to infinite possibility.*

Look at the thoughts and beliefs that keep you stuck in fear and limitation and ask yourself, 'Does it have to be this way?' Ask yourself how you want to feel, and how you want life to be. Open up to the idea that you are not your old stories – you are brand new in every moment, and anything is possible.

To anchor a higher frequency, the denser frequencies you hold in your cells must be seen and alchemized – suppressed emotions, old wounds, programming and conditioning, beliefs and thoughts that do not serve you, and patterns and ways of being, from all lifetimes.

And so, no longer ignoring and suppressing your fears, you begin to face them. As you face and feel them, you let them move through you, bringing light into the darkest corners of your being. This is the healing process that is happening as a natural by-product of the ascension.

Even when you feel lost or stuck, know that you're never actually stuck. You're just having an opportunity to feel it all and learn to love yourself. You're mastering the art of loving yourself even when you feel the most unworthy. The lesson is to have compassion for yourself through it all, and keep coming back to your heart.

As you let go of these heavy tethers, you will find yourself feeling lighter, more trusting, more at peace... more in love with yourself, with life, with what could be. You will start noticing more things to appreciate and love around you. Feeling the energy of the Earth holding you, you will hear your soul's guidance and embody your light.

This expansive version of you has been waiting for you. It has always been available to you, just waiting for you to accept it and know that you're worthy of it.

In every cell of your being, know that it is safe to step out of the comfort zone that once felt secure. And when you let go of the past, instead of struggling and forcing your way through life, you can create new possibilities from love, imagination, and excitement... tapped into the magical elixir of your soul and your divine connection to Source.

This journey is asking you to open your heart and dare to believe in the new before you can see it. But as crazy as it sounds, something in you recognizes this tune. It's a long-forgotten melody. And something deep inside of you is stirring.

CHAPTER 4

A New Navigating System

How do you navigate the new way? When most humans venture into unknown territory, they look for a road map, some form of instruction or guide. But this ascension journey is the ultimate uncharted territory, and there is no blueprint for where you are heading.

There is no road map or template, because part of this journey involves dissolving all road maps and templates. You are going beyond where your consciousness has ever been before, and so you must let go of your desire to have directions to guide you or proof of what's on the other side. You must tune in to your own inner compass and feel your way forward energetically.

This journey is unique to each individual. Of course there are shared themes, and those on a similar path can share their journey and learnings, but you must carve your own path.

It feels like you are tiptoeing through the dark at first, with only the whispers of your heart to follow. You cannot see where you're heading, but you know there is no place for you in the old world anymore. So, you keep going.

This journey isn't just a series of physical steps anymore. It is deeply energetic. You're traveling into the depths of your being, unraveling lifetimes of programming, feeling the intensity of higher frequencies bombarding your cells, while old energies and trapped emotions are coming up to be released. And this is what shifts your physical reality.

The beautiful thing about not having a road map for your ascension journey is it empowers you to trust yourself and what you're going through… to validate your own emotions and journey… and realize *you* create how you experience your life.

This journey is no longer written in the stars. It is written by you, with every breath you take, and your footsteps create the trail. Where you are heading is beyond the prophecies of the ancients and your incarnations in the highest dimensions. You are expanding the consciousness of all existences in this multiverse.

If you feel there are few around you who are shining the light to show you the way, it is because you are the light. You are the torchbearer, holding the light – first and foremost, for yourself. And in this lifetime, you chose to light the way yourself, to lead yourself… and you wouldn't have it any other way.

> *Your light ripples out, showing others*
> *they are not alone, that it is safe, that*
> *they, too, can find their own path.*

It gives others the hope that a new way is possible. This is how humanity rises, with every soul who finds their light within. As scary as it might sound to step into unknown territory, you are ready for this. You don't want to follow the path that others have walked. You want to tune in to your own soul's melody and bring it to life. You want to discover all that you can be, and all that you are, in your unique way. And this is what is so exciting to the soul – to find your courage with every step you take.

∞

Your journey is your own, but this chapter will offer a new navigating system, a compass to help orient you in forging your unique path.

First, it is important to understand that everything is inverted in the world you have known. In the past, humans were very connected to nature and their spirit, and the way they lived was much more harmonious with the organic template of the Earth. The organic template is the purest version of this Earth, the way it was meant to be.

Today, the organic template is still intact. In fact, it is thriving – held in place by nature. Go into nature, and you will find the highest frequency, the true pace of life, the interconnectedness of it all… You will feel the undeniable presence of spirit, and this will help you tune in to your own spirit.

But humans have disconnected from this organic template, both the nature around them and their true inner nature. They have disconnected from their hearts and inner wisdom… denying their connection to the universe, the soul, and the Earth.

This disconnection happened slowly over many centuries, accelerating with the rise of the modern world. Humans built artificial constructs – cities, systems, and institutions – separating them from the natural world. These constructs supported new ideas of what it meant to make progress, be happy, and be a productive citizen of the world. Society and culture shaped and reinforced these new values, priorities, and beliefs. And with every generation, more people adopted the artificial world and its concrete jungle as the real world, even though it was a complete inversion of the organic world. Instead of living from the heart, connected to spirit, they were living from the mind.

The artificial world told them a story: You are small. You are unworthy. You must hustle. Life is hard. There will never be enough.

They internalized these messages, because that was what they saw all around them – reflected by their community, friends, family, and the news. They took these beliefs, fears, and ways of being on as fact, and they unconsciously passed them down to their children.

This is the societal programming that has caused you to buy into a specific worldview: a set of beliefs, values, and priorities. What you 'should' do. What you 'should' want. How you 'should' live. What life and this world are about. This programming is embedded in every facet of society, invisible but ever present. It is all that you have known.

From the soul's perspective, even this programming has been perfect; you chose to experience it so that you could have the experience of coming back home to your heart and creating a New Earth, your answer to this disconnection. The pendulum has swung far enough now to force people to awaken and yearn for a new way. And it is not only a return to the organic template of the Earth – it is a total upgrade, catapulting you into a new frequency of a spiritually embodied existence.

In this life, you are coming into harmony. Out of your head, into your heart. From rushing to being. From fear to trust. All of this feels counterintuitive at first, because your entire world has been wired the other way. The old patterns are like a giant magnet, trying to pull you back. You see your peers, friends, and society all rushing in one direction, and it feels crazy to resist the tide.

There is great momentum against you, so in order to spin the cycle the other way around, you almost have to stop everything and come to a standstill to steady your being, quieten the noise, and begin moving the other way.

The new navigating system in the following pages will help you begin unraveling the old and stepping into the new. Instead of living from the mind, you will begin to live from the heart. Instead of being rooted in lack and fear, making decisions from that place, you will begin to anchor into possibility and trust. Everything you experience blooms from that space, and everything you create will be touched by that frequency of limitlessness, expanding beyond your human programming. You will begin to embody the knowing of your soul.

It takes a great unlearning. The bravest becoming.

This ascension is not a linear journey. So instead of chronological steps, here are a handful of components that may come up for you. They may appear in any order; they can also happen simultaneously. This journey does not adhere to a timeline or sequence of events. Each experience is to be lived and embodied, as this is your path to knowing yourself as the light of Source.

The Lens of the Soul

To pave the path toward a new way, you must let go of everything you think you know... not only your beliefs, but the entire lens with which you navigate life. You must turn your gaze from the outside in, from seeing life through your human lens to seeing life through the lens of the soul.

The human lens sees the physical world and thinks this is all there is. And because of this, you don't readily believe in what you can't see or prove. You believe this reality is fixed, finite, and linear. You believe you are a small pawn in a gigantic universe, and that life is happening *to* you.

When you start seeing through the eyes of the soul, everything changes. The human looks at the outer reality and tries to change it. The soul looks within and knows that the change must first happen on the inside – and then the outer will shift.

The soul looks at the world and doesn't see just physicality, it sees energy. It sees reality as fluid, infinite, and multidimensional. It knows that you are consciousness. You are energy. And the reality you experience is a holographic projection of your consciousness. It shifts in response to your frequency.

Your reality morphs in response to you, every moment of every day. When you shift, the reality you perceive shifts. You don't realize this is happening, because it happens constantly, faster than the speed of light. Your mind takes all of this information and strings it together in a linear fashion so that it's digestible to you.

If you are living on autopilot, your day-to-day reality will look and feel the same, because your thoughts, fears, and patterns are on repeat. But have you noticed when your energy is different, when you are light on your feet and connected to your heart – the people you encounter, the experiences you have, and most of all, the way you feel change? You are in a higher frequency, and so you are quite literally in a different dimension.

As you awaken, you realize that you can choose how you experience life, as you exist in a quantum reality with infinite possibilities. It may seem that this physical world is all there is, but there are actually infinite timelines, versions of reality, versions of you – energetically different versions of Earth. You can break free of the old patterns and choose a new way. The moment you become aware of this, you become acutely aware of yourself. You tune in to more expansive visions of what is possible. And your reality begins rearranging itself.

Breaking Down Your Programming

Another component of this navigating system is becoming aware of when you're operating from your programming. When you have thoughts rooted in fear, limitation, or judgment, this is your programming; you are in your head. As real as these thoughts may seem, they do not have to be your truth. Your awareness stops your programming from running your life on autopilot, so you can begin creating your reality from the truth of your soul.

Your core fears and beliefs are deeply rooted from childhood and many lifetimes. Practice becoming more aware of your thoughts and fears, asking yourself, 'Is this belief true to who I am becoming and how I want to feel? Does it have to be true?'

Any time you have a thought based in limitation (i.e. 'can't,' 'won't,' 'not enough,' 'not possible'), catch yourself. Observe what reality you are feeding, or agreeing to, based on your belief system. You have a choice now – see it, feel it, heal it, and break the programming. (In Chapter 6, we will dive into how to clear this density. And in Chapter 8, we will go deeper into how to transcend your programming.)

Following Your Inner Guidance

Your soul does not exist in fear or doubt. Your soul knows who you truly are and what is possible. It exists in pure joy… and you can connect with this energy by opening your heart. Your heart is the portal to all that you are, the knowing and guidance of your soul.

And so, another component of this navigating system is to open your heart and learn to trust your heart and soul over the programming of your mind. Opening your heart is an ongoing journey, because the love in your heart expands infinitely – and where you are heading is living from the fullness of your ever-expanding heart.

Opening Your Heart

Become aware of your heart

Notice when you are feeling softer, more connected to the present moment, connected with who you are. Become aware of how it feels when your heart is soaring open – when you're looking into the eyes of someone you love or your pet… when you're in flow state, immersed in something that you absolutely love, like dancing, singing, or creating… or just that sense of peace when you're walking in nature, and you feel alive.

Set the intention to melt the walls around your heart

If you've been living in your head, you may not know what it's like to truly feel your heart. The heartaches of your past may have caused you to subconsciously build energetic walls of protection around your heart. To free your heart, you must first melt these walls.

This intention alone will set this shift in motion and bring to you the experiences, healing modalities, and nudges from your universe that will help you open your heart. There are countless modalities out there for diving into this, from inner child healing meditations, breathwork, and journaling, to somatic practices, forgiveness meditations (of self and others), various practices to regulate your nervous system, and more. You can do many of these on your own by looking up videos online or finding a practitioner near you. These modalities will help you feel your emotions, process your traumas, feel safer in your body, and learn to love yourself and your inner child.

These tools are powerful doorways into yourself, and it is best to trust the ones that you feel drawn to and the ones that seem to appear synchronistically in your life. This journey will look unique to everyone, but there is a beautiful pathway available to everyone who wants to open their heart.

Choose to drop into your heart and listen to its nudges

When you notice you're in your head, pause and take a deep breath. Come back to your center. You may find whatever gets you out of your head helps, from journaling to walking in nature, moving your body, or doing something kind for someone. But it is most powerful to simply bring awareness to your heart throughout your day, especially when you notice you are in your head. It may just take a few deep breaths to zoom out and recenter, and this will get easier the more you do it.

When you are in your heart, you will experience a place of peace, limitlessness, and trust. Even if it's for a split second. And you start wondering, *What is more real? What is more true? The voice of the mind or the voice of the heart?* When you start trusting the voice of your heart more, tuning in to your true inner being, your soul can come forward more clearly to speak to you and guide you.

You will start to hear quiet little nudges... little whispers of encouragement, comfort, or inspiration that seem to be coming from deep within. This is your soul talking to you.

At first, it might be quiet and sporadic, but the more you listen, the more you give validity to this inner voice, the more you'll recognize it. You'll hear it most when you're in your heart – when you're not trying to figure it all out, and when you're least expecting it. Sometimes, it might come to you in the shower, right before you fall asleep, or when you're listening to a beautiful song.

Start paying attention to this voice. Even though it sounds just like your own voice in your head, it feels different from the voice of your worries, doubts, and fears, because it makes you feel calm.

The voice of the soul – or heart, or higher self (it's all the same) – is your true inner guidance coming online. And unlike the voice of the programmed mind, it is gentle. It doesn't need to convince you of anything. It doesn't repeat itself with excuses or arguments. It doesn't yell at you loudly. It speaks simply and quietly, carrying an energy of love, encouragement, and trust: 'It's all working out.' 'Take this step; it'll be exciting.' 'You can do it.' 'Know that everything happens for a reason.'

The voice of the mind can sound more like: 'If you don't do this, you'll fall behind.' 'You can't do it.' 'You're not doing enough.' The energy underneath is one of force or lack.

Trust your path. You don't need to rush or force it. When you are trying to figure it out, you are in your head. When you relax and let yourself enjoy the moment and just be with whatever is in front of you, you are opening up your heart.

> *Hearing your soul's guidance isn't a special 'gift.'*
> *It is possible for everyone.*

As you start to listen to your heart and follow its little nudges, you will be able to hear it more clearly. You will open up to a new frequency of existence and begin to trust the voice of your soul rather than the voice of your mind.

Try to approach this journey with gentleness. It doesn't have to be a disciplined mission of self-improvement; that is missing the point. Let yourself soften, and trust that your journey is unfolding in absolute perfection.

Using Your Emotions as a Compass

You can also use your emotions as a guiding compass. The emotions of curiosity and excitement are signals from your soul, guiding you toward your highest path. Orient your inner compass to follow these nudges of excitement. When you feel that excitement in your heart, it is an indication of the direction your soul is nudging you to go.

This isn't about putting pressure on yourself to choose the one big thing you're excited about. This is about following the tiny little nudges of excitement, especially the smallest nudges and seemingly insignificant options you have throughout the day. For example, you might feel a nudge to go for a walk, open this book, go to a new café, or call a friend. Or you might feel bigger nudges, like to start painting again, record a video, write down some ideas… Whatever pings you as the most exciting thing you could do in that moment, follow that.

It is normal to feel excited about something, while also noticing fear coming up. But the fear of doing something that you want to do, deep down, is a good sign. Your soul is nudging you outside your comfort zone. This energy only feels like fear because you hold beliefs that do not align with your soul's truth, like 'I'm not good enough.' But keep meeting this fear and take the step anyway. The fear will alchemize and shift into excitement.

Many people think that they need to overcome their self-doubt and figure out how something's going to work out *before* they take a step forward – and this is where they are mistaken. The only way to truly face your fear and give yourself a chance to overcome it is to take a step forward first. It doesn't happen the other way around. You must leap first, and then the next step will show itself.

If an idea moves you, you'll know it in the way it lights a spark in your heart, raises goosebumps on your skin, and makes you daydream about it with joy. This is your soul communicating with you.

This is just a nudge – it doesn't have to be practical at this stage. Your mind will want to see how it can work logistically before it gives it a chance to bloom on its own. But know that many of the most exciting nudges from your soul will *not* look practical. Follow them anyway. Indulge your curiosity. Allow yourself to play in it. Don't worry about whether or not you're wasting your time, or where this is going to lead next. Consistently show up for this thread of excitement, knowing that *being* in the frequency of excitement is what opens all the doors.

When you follow the breadcrumbs of excitement, you are following the guidance of your soul. There is truly no wrong path you can take, and your excitement opens the floodgates to more ideas, synchronicities, ease, and abundance.

Humans want to control their path and know the end goal before they begin, but the soul's journey is the opposite of that. This is about following the nudges, moment by moment, without needing to know where it's taking you or attaching to how it will turn out. Follow these nudges one by one, simply for the sake of excitement and curiosity, and this will create more momentum.

If nothing feels really exciting to you, this may be because your mind is putting too much pressure on figuring out what you're meant to do. Your mind may be trying to come up with your one big purpose or direction. And this will keep you stuck, because you don't want to choose the wrong thing.

You might find yourself interested in a variety of options, but there isn't one that stands out. Or you might find yourself paralyzed and not feeling moved by anything, and so you distract and numb yourself.

If you don't feel any excitement or desire in life, it may be because your body is stressed, exhausted, in fight-or-flight mode, and you are numbing your emotions. Know that there is always excitement, inspiration, and love in your heart – but you may feel disconnected from it.

When this happens, it is important to first tend to your body, regulate your nervous system, and fill your cup. You can rest, journal, sit in nature, disconnect from your devices for a few hours or a day, move your body, change up your morning routine, and so on. Ask your body what it needs. Allow yourself to rest and replenish yourself, without rushing to what's next.

Are there any difficult emotions or fears you've been avoiding? Sit with them, and let yourself feel them fully. Sometimes, it takes time to feel the spark again. But know that it hasn't disappeared – it's still there, waiting for you to reconnect.

Again, this practice isn't about deciding upon your purpose or direction for the rest of your life. It's about following the frequency of excitement, because it is a signpost, leading you to the next synchronicity, the next fork in the path, and the next expansion of who you are. And sometimes it will take you to a lesson or trigger, something you needed to feel or see in order to break through. You might think you are stuck, but this is just an opportunity to love yourself in this space and heal that part of you that judges yourself. It is all absolutely perfect; nothing that happens is out of place or not meant for you. Each step, if you stay open and curious, will take you to your highest expansion… on a path even more magical than anything you can plan.

∞

This concept was one of the guiding lights that I believe helped my path bloom in extraordinary ways.

A few months after I left my full-time job in Silicon Valley, I decided to consciously follow the nudges of excitement and curiosity. Many were seemingly insignificant, like spending more time outside with my bare feet on the grass, or listening to a podcast interview of someone who had paved an unconventional path to follow their heart.

One of the bigger nudges was to explore more books and alternative videos about spirituality and the nature of this quantum universe. From around the age of 10, I'd been interested in mind-bending topics like consciousness, the universe, and manifestation, but this time I went a lot deeper… journaling, reflecting, and applying these concepts to my daily life.

My writing began to flow more easily, and I started a little blog (another nudge I followed), which helped me drum up the courage to share some of my reflections there, and later on social media. At the time, I didn't see myself as a 'real' writer, but this felt like a step toward one of my childhood dreams.

As exciting as it was, though, it brought me face to face with my greatest doubts and self-judgments:

~ 'No one's going to read this.'
~ 'This is so cheesy.'
~ 'Who am I to think I can do this?'
~ 'What am I doing with my life?'

In those early years, doubt was my most constant companion, walking alongside me with every step, blocking the door, tripping me into waves of vulnerability that made me lie paralyzed in the fetal position, wishing I could just hide. I still had one foot in my old career, doing freelance consulting and working remotely for tech companies, but with every day, this felt more monotonous and suffocating to me. I couldn't see myself doing it for another year, let alone five years, but it gave me some financial security, and the thought of quitting felt impossible.

At the time, I didn't believe my writing could pay the bills. It was still such a vulnerable part of me, the rawest glimpse of my essence and heart, and I was terrified of being so transparently seen and judged. I didn't have confidence in my choice to pave my own path, and I had no idea where all of this was leading… or whether I'd fall flat on my face.

But despite my fears, in the quiet hours I felt enthralled by the joy of writing and exploring my consciousness. Against all logic, I believed this path was leading me somewhere worth exploring. And deep down, I knew I had to keep going to find out.

Another nudge I followed was to buy a sketchbook and start drawing again. This led to oil painting for the first time in a decade, something I had loved to do from childhood. I didn't want to become a full-time artist, so this is an example of a nudge I followed for the sake of fun, without attachment to the outcome. But it helped me stretch my imagination and explore another way of creating from the heart.

Though I didn't know it at the time, a year later I would be 'randomly' invited to participate in a local art show in the city, which motivated me to paint a series of paintings in a short amount of time. Another year later, these paintings would end up in my first book – a full-color hardcover with my own artwork on the cover and displayed throughout the pages, along with words channeled from my heart.

None of this was planned with any foresight. It was all a result of daring to follow the nudges, one baby step at a time, despite the fear. At the same time, it felt divinely orchestrated by my soul.

Around this time, I stumbled upon an old journal that I kept at the age of 8. I will never forget the goosebumps I felt when I read what I had written on one of the pages: 'When I grow up, I will be an author and artist.' In my early career, I may have felt like I lost my way... but everything had been leading me to this full-circle moment.

Looking into the Mirrorverse

Another fundamental component of this navigating system is viewing your outer reality as a mirrorverse. Imagine this universe is a giant kaleidoscopic mirror, and everything out there is a reflection of your frequency. It is an ever-expanding, ever-changing mirrorverse, reflecting back to you all that you are.

Every being you interact with, everyone that you love, everyone that challenges you is reflecting some aspect of your own soul, because from the highest perspective, you are the only one that exists. This reality is a creation of your own consciousness, allowing you to experience physicality, interact with others, and create your reality – so that you can see yourself from different angles, know yourself more fully, and clear the parts of you that no longer align with the light that you are.

The greatest healing modality is your daily life, as your experiences bring you exactly what you need to see and feel for your journey. For example, you might have a conversation that triggers something in you – an insecurity, fear, or unwanted emotion. The human part of you will react and go straight into victimhood or blame, withdrawing or lashing out. Instead, recognize the trigger and take a moment to sit with what it is bringing up. What disempowering beliefs are you holding on to? They are being illuminated, because they want to be seen and let go.

This physical realm on Earth offers you the richest, most multifaceted way possible for you to experience your consciousness through interacting with your reality. Without this physical reality, you would not be able to fully know yourself, because you need the contrasting variety of reflections to see yourself more deeply. This life allows you to feel it all. You can see what it's like to love and feel joy, or get hurt and forgive… Every experience allows you to look deeper into the beliefs you hold, and every interaction lets you see what qualities you like or don't like in others. All of this is here for you.

When you start seeing your reality as a mirror, you'll see that everything that happens, catches your attention, or makes you feel something in your daily life holds a reflection for you. Everything is a gift, offering you a chance to see yourself even more clearly… a sign from your soul, a message.

This doesn't mean you are responsible for everything that happens outside of you, especially to others. Every soul is walking their own journey, choosing their path. But if a situation brings up any emotions in you, it is there for you to see what it's making you feel about yourself and alchemize that. For example, you may have a family member who is suffering, and you feel incredibly helpless. Try as you might, nothing you say or do is helping them. The reflection for you in this experience is to allow yourself to feel the helplessness, the frustration… which will uncover the grief hiding underneath the frustration. You will realize that you cannot fix anyone, you can only offer your love and be there for them when they are receptive to help. And as hard as it is, this is calling you into a deeper level of trust – in life, in the universe, in every soul's path.

Even those who challenge you most in your life are a gift, because they allow you to dig deeper and see how they make you feel about yourself. And from there, you can decide whether this feeling, and the belief under it, aligns with the truth of who you are. For example, if someone hurts you and makes you feel bad about yourself, you might notice you feel unworthy. But this is not the truth of your soul. It needed to be triggered, so that you could feel it, look at it, and decide for yourself how you want to feel and see yourself.

To remember who you truly are, you must unlearn all that you are not. If you notice recurring patterns and cycles in your life, they are a strong indication to look more deeply into what they are reflecting for you. If you're carrying a wound, you'll continue attracting people, challenges, and experiences that trigger it. But when you start healing that wound, you'll notice that this experience no longer shows up in your life. Lessons and cycles repeat until you break down the programming that is creating them and clear them from the inside out. This allows a brand-new reality to emerge that is more aligned with the new frequency you have anchored within.

For example, someone who keeps attracting emotionally unavailable partners may look within and realize that they themselves have a deep fear of commitment. And underneath this fear is a fear of abandonment and a lack of self-worth. They may have subconsciously chosen, and attracted, partners that are emotionally unavailable, because it feels safer than the risk of a committed relationship. Instead of the usual pattern of blaming the unavailable partners, they can use this experience to look deeper into their own fear of abandonment and begin healing it at the core. Simply being aware of this fear and working on it can allow them to love themselves more and know that they are safe, which can shift their reality and open up the possibility of meeting a partner who can fully meet them.

Other people aren't your only mirrors.

Every situation, event, and experience is a mirror.
It is all happening for you – for you to feel something,
see something, shift something, and empower yourself.

Sometimes in life, terrible things happen – and this is not because you attracted them into your reality or karmically created them (this is a human way of looking at it through the lens of victimhood). The mirrorverse isn't about looking at a circumstance or situation and blaming yourself for it. It simply provides a reflection so you can look at your inner experience (emotions, reactions, or thoughts), triggered by what has happened. When you observe your inner experience, you can then see what this event is making you feel about yourself. And then you can decide: Do you want to let it disempower or empower you? Do you want to feed the story that you're a victim of it, or do you want to rise above it? If it makes you feel anything less than the Source that you are, *this* is the shadow in you that is being illuminated for you to bring back into the light.

The mirrorverse gives you reflections not only of the shadow, but also of the light that you are, allowing you to see it in yourself and embody it more fully. Everything that touches your heart – every triumph, beautiful sunset, and kindness you experience – all of this and more is a reflection of you.

This reality is your creation, and it is the way your soul communicates with you. When you see everything out there as a communication for your soul, you can no longer be a victim of your reality. You see how everything is happening for your expansion.

Reframing Challenges

Another component of this navigating system, expanding upon the mirrorverse, is changing your perspective on challenges. Challenges and physical ailments often come up to get you to look within, especially when you are ignoring what needs to be seen and felt. This is one way your soul has chosen to grow, through the feedback loop of your mirrorverse. Everything outside of you is happening to get you to go within. The more you proactively sit with your fears, look at your limiting beliefs, and feel the emotions you may have been suppressing, the fewer roadblocks and challenges you'll have to experience in your outer reality.

Going within collapses the timeline where you may have needed to experience a disruptive event or challenge to force you to look deeper. This is because you are proactively clearing what is not in alignment with your soul, allowing your outer reality to shift.

Doing the inner work can feel uncomfortable, but it is much easier than having to face challenge after challenge, constantly getting sick because you're ignoring the cues of your body and soul. Ignoring your inner world is what often leads to exhaustion, illness, and burnout.

You may still experience challenges from time to time, but they will no longer feel so big. You will see them as subtle redirections and eye-opening experiences – more opportunities for clarity and growth. They will no longer feel 'negative' to you, as you let go of your expectations around how it 'has to be' and trust that everything is happening for your highest expansion. They will resolve themselves more smoothly and easefully, because you will face them more calmly.

The next time an unexpected event happens that you normally would classify as a challenge, practice seeing it with curiosity instead of frustration or fear. Even if it takes you out of alignment momentarily, remember to breathe and return to your heart… being present with whatever emotions come up. Say to yourself, 'Oh, that's interesting. What is this showing me? There must be a reason for it.'

Shine a light on how this experience is making you feel before rushing to come up with solutions from the mind. When you feel calmer, tune in and listen to whatever your soul is telling you. It might be to relax and let it be for now. Trust that the solution will come to you. Or, it might be to take some kind of action. The more you stay calm, the more easily everything will flow. In retrospect, you will be able to see the gift in why it had to unfold this way.

Journal Prompts: Navigating Challenges

You can use these journal prompts whenever unexpected challenges or roadblocks happen, or to reflect on a challenging situation in your life now.

When you encounter a challenge, practice immediately bringing your awareness to yourself. Notice the ways you are reacting and getting in your head – and instead, take a moment to breathe. Ask yourself:

- What is this challenge making me feel in my body (physically and/or emotionally)?
- What is it making me feel about myself? Is it true? Does it have to be true?
- What beliefs do I hold that are causing me to worry about this?
- Do I actually need to fear or worry about this?
- What does my soul want to tell me?
- If this is happening for a reason, to show me something, what is it showing me?
- How would I feel, and be, if I knew for certain that it is all working out?

Nothing is a test from the universe; nothing is against you. No experience is 'negative' unless you define it to be. When you know this in your bones, you will no longer see yourself as a helpless victim of any event or experience. You will empower yourself, knowing everything is happening for you. Open up to this idea, and you will attract more experiences in your life that confirm to you that this is indeed true, until you won't doubt it anymore.

Begin to see challenges with openness and curiosity, knowing they aren't actually setbacks, but part of your highest path. This is a reframe that will change your entire relationship with life.

Unlocking the Infinite Now

A final component of this navigating system is letting go of the idea that you need to get to a destination. Even the idea that you need to navigate to get somewhere other than where you are is distorted, because ultimately, your compass should point to the peace of your heart and the oneness of this moment.

This is extremely difficult for humans to do, because there has always been a goal or destination, making you think, *When my life looks like this, then I'll be happy...* or *If I do this, then I'll be of value...*

> *When you stop resisting what's happening and become fully present in your heart, you will melt into the absolute deliciousness, connection, and abundance of life.*

You will know that there is no need to do anything but be here. And then from that place, everything else blossoms. Everything becomes effortless. There is no quest to get anywhere... just to be all that you are in this moment. And that is not a future destination. It is just a frequency you can tune in to, and it is always accessible within you.

From that place of being fully at ease, connected to your heart, spirit, and nature, you will call forth a New Earth of harmony where the artificial systems that do not serve humanity can no longer exist. And humanity will give birth to new ways of being and organic structures that are aligned with values that support the soul.

Remember, this New Earth exists now, in the quantum field where all realities exist. It exists within you. When you shift yourself, when you tune in to this frequency and embody it – you bring it forth through your heart. And your holographic reality morphs to mirror to you the light you have anchored within. The deeper you journey within, the greater the heights you experience as you expand into all that you are.

CHAPTER 5

Journeying into Becoming Everything

The components for navigating the new way that we have just explored ultimately lead to remembering, reclaiming, and becoming all that you are. What does it mean to truly know all that you are, and why has it been so hard for humans to go there?

The tremendous leap into becoming all that you are starts with opening your heart to this concept: You are Source. You are Everything. You are God. Whatever you want to call it.

This concept has been alluded to and danced around in many different ways throughout your history, but it has never been fully claimed, believed, and embodied at its purest truth and frequency. Over centuries, your texts and philosophies have touched on the idea that you are one, you are connected to everything, and everything is energy. This idea has resonated with many civilizations, philosophies, and religions. Many messengers have come to the world with it. Even your quantum physicists have explored it. And it has continued coming up throughout time and across many modalities and languages, because it has resonated with you at a soul level.

But this truth has been mistranslated and misconceived. Though the original messages from Source have been pure, they have been distorted over time because of mistranslations in language and also manipulation by those in power. Many religions and civilizations have perpetuated the idea that God is outside of you. This teaching has some distortion, because it makes people think they have to put their power and trust outside of them – in gods or a God they believe is above them and separate from them.

Those in the highest echelons of power have been keen to perpetuate this, for they have been pulling the strings for centuries to keep humanity small and easy to control. And they have found that one of the most effective ways to control humanity is through manipulating the information that is fed into our minds and hearts. (From the highest perspective, it's important to clarify that there is no 'they.' You created this experience as a soul, so that you could expand into all that you are and free yourself again. However, in this dimension on Earth, there exists a tangible experience of being controlled and oppressed by others.)

Religion also gained momentum because billions of people found strength and comfort in praying to a God outside of them – and for many, this actually helped them open their hearts, trust, and surrender. It served humanity in many ways, because it gave you the hope that something outside of you can answer your prayers, guide you, and comfort you on your worst days. It gave humanity the beautiful belief in something greater – the idea that there is more to life than you can see, which is true. It has helped your species endure the darkest of nights. Religion has been a powerful stepping stone for humanity on the journey into the full realization of God. And so, there is no right or wrong with any path, as every soul chooses whatever they are meant to experience in this life.

Throughout history, the most groundbreaking ideas that changed how we view life, ourselves, and the world as we know it were first thought to be crazy. They were vehemently rejected or ridiculed for years, even decades, before being accepted by the collective consciousness as truth.

Now, you are able to move beyond your past programming, because your consciousness is expanding, and you're able to actually begin to *embody* the oneness that you are. There is a big difference between resonating with the idea that you are one and fully embodying the knowing that you are one – that you are God. The idea that you are not just a child of God, but you are God – you are consciousness experiencing itself – may be one of the most radical yet for humanity to consider.

There have been centuries of programming around the word 'God,' both positive and negative. From ancient times, humans have attempted to understand God by imagining God as human-like, with emotions and grudges. They have spoken about God's vengeance, anger, and mercy – but this is the result of humans trying to personify an energy that is absolutely pure and cannot be brought down into conditions or emotions. God is a frequency, an energy. God is everything. The purest frequency of God is the highest love, the Oneness of all there is. God is the light and also the shadow that has forgotten it is the light. It is the energy of all of existence.

Today, many who see themselves as spiritual but not religious may not like to use the word 'God' because of the religious connotations and centuries of portrayals of God as a man in the sky, someone to be feared, someone to revere. It's time to let go of the stereotypical, mythological, and religious portrayals of God that have been passed down from human mind to human mind.

If you find resistance to the word 'God' in this text, you can substitute whatever word(s) you wish that feel expansive to your consciousness. You are Source, embodied. You are your universe, the entire multiverse. These are all true, and yet there is a powerful energy in saying it even more bluntly and clearly, 'I am God.' To be clear, this is not about claiming this from the ego. You must expand beyond the constraints of your human mind and realize you are more than this lifetime, this human existence.

And God is real, but not separate from you. Think of it as consciousness, energy, and pure light. In this light, you will know yourself as the most brilliant unconditional love, which is exponentially greater than any love you have felt in your lifetime. It is a love beyond what the human mind can hold. It is the love that unites you with all that you are and all that is. And when you feel this love, this Oneness, this light, all the separation disappears – and you know without a doubt that this *is* you.

You are light. You are love.
You are the universe. All of it is you.

In this lifetime, you are breaking down all the ideas that keep you in separation, as lesser than. It might help to think of it this way: Little You is this human personality – your name, this lifetime, this body, and all that you identify with. Of course, Little You is not actually little. You are so much more than you know. But you can think of yourself, this human personality, as Little You.

Big You is consciousness and all that you truly are. It is Source, Oneness, God, the universe, energy, whatever you want to call it. But remember, there is no separation, and so Little You is Big You.

When you just identify as Little You, you miss seeing the whole picture of your connectedness to it all. But in this lifetime, you are starting to shift your consciousness to see through the eyes of Big You. And Big You doesn't have the fears, worries, or doubts of Little You. Big You is in pure peace, the purest frequency of bliss and unconditional love.

When you start tuning in to the energy of Big You, you activate the codes of your inner knowing, limitlessness, and unity consciousness. These codes have always been within you, but now you're giving yourself permission to unlock them, knowing that you are worthy of embodying this frequency.

There is liberation in letting go of all the past programming and warped conceptions, allowing yourself to feel the purity and power of your connection to all of creation. And this is what allows you to feel the truest energy of God that weaves through you, and through it all. This is what allows you to appreciate the full magnificence of God's energy and your true nature.

Many of you have not allowed yourself to accept that you are God, because it feels too egotistical to say such a thing. But this is not about hierarchy or ego. This journey is not about playing God, with the energy of 'I'm so special, look at me.' You have done this in other lifetimes, even in the higher dimensions, when you've been a priestess, a sage, a leader... lifetimes where you may have been connected to your spirit, but your ego carried you off-balance.

In those lifetimes, you still needed something – to be seen and loved, or be in power and control. You may have been playing 'gods' and 'goddesses' through your ego, without knowing yourself as God in your heart. There is a massive difference between the two. You were still looking outward to gain what you felt you were missing inside.

It's beautiful to feel your power, your magic, your inherent worth. But when you fully see this in yourself in its purest form, you see it in all others. And so, you won't use it to put yourself above others. All beings are on the journey of knowing themselves as God experiencing God.

It's time for humanity to stop seeing itself as small. After centuries of being told you were small, it's scary to consider the exact opposite, especially if you also believe those who think they're 'all that' are full of it. But this is about your connection and union with everything. The animals, the blades of grass, every drop of water – all of it is God. You are all of it, and so is everyone else. All of you are reflections of each other, walking yourselves home into the remembering that you are everything.

When you truly embody the energy of all that you are, you will no longer seek anything outside of yourself. You won't need to be seen a certain way, because you fully see yourself. This embodiment cannot be reached through the mind. If you try to know it through your mind, it will be impossible to fully grasp, and you will only see it through the lens of your ego.

You can only feel the Oneness that you are through your heart. The portal of your heart is where your divinity meets your humanity.

When you journey into your heart, you will feel the Oneness that you are, your infinite love, and eternal nature – because it is the heart that has always known you are one.

This is the ultimate journey into knowing yourself as everything: the infinite, the witness, the light, and the shadow – integrating all aspects of yourself into one.

You are worth it. Worth discovering the opposite of feeling unworthy, not good enough, and alone. Worth playing in limitlessness, instead of limitations. Worth opening your eyes to the truth of who you are – because it's the greatest cosmic giggle to forget where you came from and trick yourself into thinking you are a tiny speck in a gigantic universe.

Once you truly awaken to who you are, you will laugh at how much you had forgotten, laugh at all the illusions you believed to be true.

The Loneliness of Being Everything

From the human perspective, trying to grasp the idea that you are everything might bring up feelings of loneliness as you contemplate that you are the only one here… that there is nothing else but you. It is all you. Infinitely you.

You, me, everyone – we are experiencing ourselves as fractals of consciousness, journeying into the remembering that we are one. And it can feel incredibly isolating, this existential loneliness of, 'Oh, I've just been talking to myself this whole time.' Even this book is a message from another aspect of you, one that you brought to yourself at this precise moment in life so that you could see or feel something within yourself. Only you can realize what that is for you.

But this concept only feels lonely or overwhelming because you are viewing it from your human mind, and it is too big to comprehend with the mind. When you collapse all separation and become everything, there will be no loneliness – only the most beautiful, all-encompassing connection with all there is. It is the purest existence, where everything is whole and there is nothing but the bliss of Oneness. You will know that you are never alone.

And so, this journey into all that you are has to simultaneously come with the opening of your heart.

Anchoring the Light Activation: Opening Your Heart to Your Divine Connection

Go into nature and feel the sun on your face, the grass kissing your bare feet... and allow yourself to tune in to the peace of nature, the presence, the frequency around you. Reconnect with the organic template of the Earth, of creation.

Nature holds the highest frequency steady, allowing you to receive it and expand your own frequency whenever you need to. When you tune in to it and let yourself just be, you will begin to feel your heart soften. You will feel your mind quieten as you open up to your connection with everything around you.

After a while, you may feel like you've entered another dimension. It may look exactly the same as it always does, at first glance. But it will be as if you've melted into another layer of depth within yourself. And through your presence, your awareness, you will find a new frequency, where everything feels more vibrant, more alive.

When you contemplate that you are God, this can bring up all the emotions and beliefs that you hold in your body that are opposite to that statement. When you say, 'I am everything,' and yet you hold the beliefs that you not worthy, not good enough, that you are small, all of this density will come up to be seen and felt.

All of the beliefs that hold you in separation must come up to be cleared for you to fully know yourself as all that you truly are. We will explore how to do this in the next chapter. This is part of the ascension process – letting go of limiting beliefs so that you can unite all the aspects of your soul and dimensions within yourself.

Why does the human feel scared to open up to this? It is the unknown. It has always been scary to step into the unknown when you feel unworthy, when you don't trust life. It is comforting to know there are others alongside you who are also struggling or whom you can reach out to for support. But when you realize all of them are you, this places a giant responsibility on your shoulders.

You might think, *I don't know enough, I can't be it all. You're telling me there's no one else but me, and no one can save me… only me. This leaves me hanging, because I believe I'm not good enough, and I need help on my path.* Or, *Who am I to say I am everything, when all I feel is my brokenness?*

But it is your programming, trauma, and shadow that you are feeling. It is not who you truly are.

You must expand far beyond your human lens. You have always been guided by your soul, your highest self, all aspects of your infinite soul. You have always been the one guiding yourself. As you claim this, you will see that you have all the answers within – access to everything you need… because you are everything.

VISIONS FOR THE NEW EARTH

The air is fizzy, and every breath I take feels so delicious, as it energizes all the cells of my body. This pure prana *nourishes my being, calming my mind, sinking me deeper into presence.*

It has never felt so delicious to just be. *There is no tension in my body, no resistance to the moment, no worries of the past or the future. Just the pure ecstasy of being alive. My heart is flying open, flooding with more love than I've ever felt before.*

Glimpses of Oneness

You may have glimpsed these moments where you've felt your connection to it all. Perhaps in childhood, in nature, or in meditation… when you've visited these dimensions within yourself where all you feel is love. Love, which is what you are. And the pure bliss of the moment is so delicious, it is absolutely complete. You do not need anything else.

Holding the knowing of all that you are, your connectedness to it all, means no longer seeing anything as out of place. From the infinite perspective of your soul, nothing can be done to you. Nothing can be taken from you. Everything is flowing in perfect orchestration. You begin to see every experience, every being in your life, everything that happens in your reality through the eyes of God… the eyes of love, the purest unconditional love that you are.

Everything fundamentally changes when you hold this frequency of Oneness. You begin living as the love that you are, knowing there is nothing but love.

You are learning to walk through the world remembering, knowing, and living as the oneness that you are, no longer just identifying as this human and all that you have known yourself to be up until now.

There may be times on your journey when you receive glimpses of this knowing through unexplainable experiences of spirit or the divinity that you are. One day it happened to my husband, Joel.

Upon waking one morning, my husband had one of the most profound spiritual experiences of his life, and it lasted for only a split second. He later described it to me.

In that moment while lying in bed, no longer asleep, but just waking up with his eyes still closed, he experienced himself as pure light. It was the most real, potent, experience of being light – not just thinking he was light, not just imagining it, but *experiencing* himself as an electric current of light. There was no thought, no body, no 'him' anymore, just weightless, pure bliss. It could have been a split second or an eternity – the purest experience of timelessness he had ever had.

After that, he felt himself drop back into his body, into the density of this realm. He told me it was the most tangible experience of his true spirit, and it felt more real than life itself. It wasn't a dream or astral traveling. It felt like he was being shown his true form, and something about it was uncannily familiar. He said words failed to fully describe the experience, but that feeling, that remembrance, has stayed with him. He knows it's not something he can recreate – it just happened, one 'random' day.

I like to think of it as a gift from his soul, another breadcrumb on the path to help him remember who he is.

> *Your soul leaves breadcrumbs on the path of life, and each one that you uncover unlocks something inside you.*

Each one has served to get you to this moment. They can come in the form of profound spiritual experiences, sparkling gems from the universe, but mostly they come in the seemingly random or mundane – a conversation, a line from a book, a song you overhear. A new friend or a kind stranger you meet. Little synchronicities. And often, they come in the form of your greatest struggles, the challenges that bring you to your knees. Even these, *especially* these, are gifts from your soul – because they make you dig deep and feel something, see something, and heal something that you wouldn't otherwise have known.

∞

You will see that all of your lifetimes of thinking you aren't good enough, hating yourself, and thinking you are small have served you. They've served you, because even when you felt at your worst, you never stopped looking for your light. Even when you felt utterly lost and in despair, you never stopped reaching for love, for yourself, for more of yourself.

And now, you are remembering you have never been truly lost. You have never been alone. It has only felt this way because the density you exist in creates such a convincing illusion of separation. And this realm has felt unbearably heavy and hard for humans.

Now, you are remembering and coming to know the Oneness that you are – and this is the ultimate gift. It is the opposite of what you have endured across eons of lifetimes. You have been carrying the deep soul despair of not knowing who you are or what you're meant to do, when you have been it all. But how could you appreciate all that you were if you didn't know what it felt like to experience the polar opposite?

Thinking you are nothing.

Thinking you are alone in the dark.

Thinking something's wrong with you.

Thinking no one likes you, no one loves you.

Now, you're stepping into seeing the light in yourself and becoming it again, embodied in this physical form. And because of this, all that you are will forever be changed. You are creating a new level of depth and vibrancy to consciousness that will ripple out across all space and time, all dimensions.

It is your human experience that has added this depth to the fabric of consciousness, this depth that allows love to expand even more.

It is you, and all that you have been across all your lifetimes, especially the lifetimes where you felt the farthest from your light. It is this life you are living now. This is what is changing consciousness forevermore.

Would any of this exist without you?

No.

This is what you chose to create.

You are the consciousness that created this entire reality. You are the consciousness that created this multiverse. You are the one who is creating it all. All of you are, because you are all one. You are all unique and experiencing life separately in these bodies, and yet your consciousness, your energy, is one. And so, from the highest perspective, you are *it*. And you – *you* – have created it all.

You have created this reality, but you have also created infinite timelines and realities that extend in all directions across space and time, across all dimensions. This is your convergence point, remembering who you are, and becoming all that you are.

You are unifying with God by remembering that you are already one with God. The magnitude of this, the fact that you are alive at this time on Earth, is profound. What are the chances? What a miracle it is, to be here in this precise blip of time – to take part in the ascension of your multiverse.

And yet, at the same time, it is destined. Of course you are here. What is the point of it all, otherwise?

And it is done.

CHAPTER 6

The Dance of Light and Shadow

There is another reason why Oneness is a concept humanity wasn't ready to fully grasp until now: accepting that you are everything means accepting both the light and shadow of the human experience. This chapter explores what the shadow is, why it's important to integrate it, and how to clear the density in your being to anchor more of your light.

Until now, many of you have understood this idea that you are one as a feel-good concept: 'We are one, *kumbaya*...' But now that you are stepping into the full embodiment of this knowing, you are realizing it is much more weighted than that.

To accept that you are one with it all is to accept the full polarity of light and dark that exists – in this human experience, and across all dimensions, all your existences. This requires your mind to grapple with a heavy truth. If you are one with everything, this means you are one with even the darkest shadows, the most heinous acts, the most evil things that you can possibly conceive. These, too, are part of the fabric of consciousness.

The human heart is beautiful, and it struggles to comprehend why terrible things can happen and be done to people. And the pain accumulated over lifetimes is so great, the extent of evil that exists so unfathomable and unforgivable, that the idea of even looking at it is too much.

This is why you must expand beyond the human lens and see it through the eyes of the soul, knowing that you have been it all, across the kaleidoscope of infinite lives – you have been the perpetrator and the victim, and everything in between. From the soul's perspective, it is just consciousness experiencing all that it is, and all that it can be; there is nothing that is truly wrong or bad.

This isn't about condoning the darkness that exists, saying it's okay and rolling over in submission to it. It isn't about trying to ignore or overpower it either, for that isn't possible. It's about coming into your heart, illuminating the darkness with your awareness... no longer being a victim to it, but meeting it eye to eye and seeing the balance of it all.

It is the human perspective that wants to judge things as good or bad. But when you view life through the lens of victimhood, seeing yourself or others as victims, you remain trapped in a lower frequency of seeing life as happening to you. To free yourself from this takes opening up to the perspective that life is happening *for* you. Everything, whether you perceive it as good or bad, is happening for the highest expansion of your soul. And this is what releases you from the grip of victimhood and into empowerment – the empowerment to transcend the old and create a new way.

> *Only by fully facing the shadow*
> *and illuminating it will you ease the*
> *suffering and pain on the planet.*

And only when you can do this can you bring light into the darkest areas of the world. Only then can you harmonize and transcend it all.

You came here to fully experience all facets of consciousness, and this includes the dark and the light. Even when you look at those who are suffering the most – you are seeing only one tiny fractal of their infinite soul. Other aspects of their soul are simultaneously experiencing the greatest joy and bliss in the most magical realities and dimensions. At the same time, they are one with Source; they never left. It is all happening at once.

In the frequency of Source, there is only pure love. This love encompasses all there is, including the shadow. Here, the shadow aspect is fully integrated as one with the light. It looks like light. It *is* light. Only when you bring it down into the lower dimensions, into separation, does the shadow become more visible. This is because you slow down the vibration and drop into density. If you speed up the vibration, the shadow looks like pure light, because that's what it is.

In the densest realms, the darkness had to exist so that the light could shine even more brightly. The contrast allowed the light to be seen. Without the experience of the shadow, you would not have fully appreciated the light.

But now you are collectively choosing to move beyond needing to be immersed in such density in order to grow as souls. You are realizing that you can expand in new ways, through the light and integrated shadow.

In this ascension, you are unifying the higher dimensions, where such wide spectrums of polarity do not exist. Even in the highest dimensions, a bit of polarity still exists so that you can have a variety of experiences, but there, you do not choose to play in the darkness but in the lighter energies. There is a greater connection with your spirit and Source, and it is much easier to live in harmony when all beings are free from fear and disconnection.

The knowing of where humanity is heading has come through more as I have begun walking the journey of becoming a mother. As I write this book, I am pregnant with our first child. About a year before we conceived, Joel and I started connecting with the souls of our future children. It has been absolutely breathtaking to feel their radiant energy and sheer excitement to experience life on Earth with us.

My first ever communication with this baby was the most tangible experience of spirit I had ever felt. I put my hands on my womb and invited the energy of my future child in.

'Hi, Mama!'

I immediately heard a high-pitched voice in my ear, crystal-clear, instantly bringing me to tears. I felt the most brilliant golden light flooding through my body.

'I picked you! I can't wait! I'm so excited!'

The energy of this child was bouncing with excitement to come to Earth to be with me and Joel.

The moment I thought of Joel, I felt a rush of the most powerful love and awe for him, through our child's eyes. It was like our child was exclaiming at the top of their lungs, 'That's my *dad*!'

I was flooded with their awe for the soul, the man, the father that Joel will be.

'He makes me feel so safe and loved and warm and I can't wait to play, play, play!'

Whenever I tune in to the souls of our future children, I can feel the energy of the New Earth they are so excited to come here for. And on many occasions when I tune in to them, their higher selves come through, sounding much older and wiser than their childhood selves. The following is one of the many messages their higher selves have given me, and humanity:

The young children and new souls being born now are no longer choosing to play in the lower dimensions and learn their soul lessons from a place of fear or lack. They are coming in simply to be here, already knowing the light that they are... connected to the light of Source that they are, without distortion, without imprints. They want to experience themselves as love, joy, and spirit in human form – and their high frequency is bringing an unprecedented amount of light to the Earth.

Their generation and the generations beyond will bring this frequency to the Earth where the shadow once was, because you have collectively chosen to transmute the shadow and bring it into the light. The hearts of humanity have been calling for a brighter light, and this is the frequency the new generations are bringing in, to expand like a web around the Earth and fill the hearts who have been in pain... to fill the Earth with more love than ever before.

Just as you chose to come into this life exactly at the moment you were born, for this time on Earth, these children are choosing to come in, exactly when they're meant to come in. Not a moment sooner or later. It is divinely perfect.

The generation being born now are not waiting until the Earth has shifted and everyone has ascended to come in. There will be later generations that will do this, and their reason for being will be slightly different. But this generation chose to come in for this moment, to be part of this pivotal time on Earth.

They are creating a domino effect, and the momentum picks up as they tip the scale; the frequency of the planet rises higher every time one of these souls is born. From the moment their energy comes into the womb, they bring this frequency to their parents, their families, their world.

They are the bringers of the light, just as you are for your generation.

They did not want to just experience being the light. They already know they are the light; they are experiencing this as Source.

They wanted to experience anchoring the light, and to bring the light you must go into a place that is less bright than the light. Otherwise you cannot have the experience of bringing the light.

This is what is happening through each and every one of you. Every soul, young and old — you are anchoring the light in your unique way.

∞

To anchor the light, you must first make room in your cellular body to hold more light. And this requires clearing the density in your body.

Clearing Density

You clear the density in your body by alchemizing and integrating your shadow. What does this mean?

You hold the entire spectrum of consciousness in your body, including the memories of everything that you have experienced in this lifetime and all lifetimes. In this ascension process, all the density that you hold in your body is coming up to be seen, felt, and alchemized – all your fears and traumas, childhood wounds, suppressed emotions, programming, limiting beliefs, and ways of being that no longer serve you.

The goal is not to anchor the light while ignoring the shadow within. This journey is about anchoring the light by witnessing and sitting with your shadow. Clearing this density is a process that happens naturally as you experience your day-to-day life, but you can also dive into it and approach it more intentionally.

As a by-product of this ascension, your fears and beliefs are coming up for you to feel and witness, whether you realize it or not. This is because more light is flooding in, shaking to the surface whatever density you hold in your being.

> *When fears or heavier emotions are triggered,*
> *they give you an opportunity to see and feel*
> *what may have been hidden from you.*

Simply feeling these fears and emotions allows them to begin to shift. This process is more effective when you do it consciously – that is, when you recognize the trigger as an invitation to sit with the emotions arising in you, without resistance or judgment. As we explored in Chapter 4, this is your soul communicating with you through your mirrorverse, allowing you to heal your wounding.

Why is it important to sit with your emotions when they are triggered? In spiritual and personal development circles, many tell you to look at the limiting beliefs and thoughts you are carrying to alchemize them. This is powerful, but you can go a layer deeper. Beneath the thought is the emotion charging it – and it may be a wound or suppressed emotion you have been carrying from life to life. And underneath your unhealed wounds is your pure essence: your soul. To get to the clarity of your soul, you must feel your emotions to alchemize and clear the trapped density attached to them.

Anchoring the Light Activation: Clearing Density

Here's what you can do when an emotion or fear is triggered in you:

Bring your awareness into your being by breathing deeply and noticing where this emotion or energy feels strongest in your body. Is it a heat in your chest, a tightening in your throat, a fogginess in your head, an uneasiness in your belly?

Continuing to breathe deeply, give this emotion space to be fully felt. You might notice it getting stronger or changing in energy. For example, anger may give way to reveal a heavy sadness beneath. You may feel like crying, screaming into a pillow, or breathing heavily, and this is wonderful, as it releases stuck energy and allows it to move through you.

Feeling your emotions fully, with awareness, is different from getting lost in the emotions and stories that your mind is telling you. For example, if you are lost in your emotions, you may judge yourself for feeling bad, thinking this must mean you're behind or not doing enough. To clear this energy, it is best to allow yourself to fully feel whatever you're feeling, with compassion for yourself. Imagine traveling into the depths of it. Sit with the energy itself, without judging yourself for feeling this way.

It's most effective to sit with your emotions right when they are triggered, bringing awareness to them the moment they start arising in your being instead of when you're thinking about what happened hours later. For example, if someone says something that makes you angry, notice the quickening of your breath, the pounding of your heart. Bring your awareness to your inner world, while watching the outer world. Feel whatever is arising, and sit with it. You might need to excuse yourself and step outside. Or you might try this right after the interaction is over, or even in the moment – while the other person is talking.

Alchemizing the emotion is less effective when you're reflecting about it hours later, because it has become a memory you are reliving in your head, though it still helps to allow yourself to feel whatever is coming up and move some energy.

I do this practice whenever a charged emotion is triggered in me and I'm able to catch myself in it. One day, I woke up to a couple hurtful and judgmental comments on a post I wrote, and this triggered my fear of not being good enough. So I sat with this energy, letting myself feel the heat in my heart, the tightening of my throat. The more I sat with it without resistance, the more emotion welled up in me... and I felt the pain of the times in my life when I hadn't felt good enough... the frustration of being rejected and made fun of... the fear of failure and being misunderstood. And underneath this pain and frustration, I found grief.

This grief showed me the weight of this energy from lifetime after lifetime of being rejected for being myself – all the lifetimes when I'd felt small, invisible, and lost. This was a collective energy, lodged deep in my psyche from all of my existences.

Something shifted when I let myself be with this energy, with awareness and compassion for myself. Light illuminated the shadows of this repressed energy, bringing it back into my heart, into love.

The wound is still there, but it's much less raw than before. I sit with it every time it comes up, but each time, it feels lighter. Now I rarely notice any negative comments on my posts – and if I do, they don't have any power over me because I don't take them personally. Most of all, I cleared the majority of my fear of being seen, and I began to share my writing more freely and unfiltered.

This is how you heal yourself at a quantum level, casting your light to yourself, to all versions of yourself, across all lifetimes. When you see it all, you will have compassion for yourself, knowing there's no way you could have overcome this earlier. You did not know how. But now, you have the ability to bring the light in. Some part of you that has always felt wounded will heal, and you will feel a little bit more whole, for the first time perhaps.

∞

With the bigger energies, you may feel you are revisiting the same fear or wound over and over again. These fears and heavy emotions are tied to deeply rooted beliefs, patterns, and wounds you've carried across many lifetimes. They are more difficult to unravel, but every time they come up, you clear another layer.

This is why you may at times feel overwhelming emotions that don't seem proportional to what's happening in your current situation. Your daily triggers or struggles in life are giving you an opportunity to feel and clear not only the emotions around the current situation, but energies you've carried over multiple lifetimes.

Past lives are actually simultaneous lives, because everything is happening now. The energy of all the lives you're simultaneously living exists in you now. And so you are feeling, and clearing, entire templates of density from all your lives.

To clear them, you don't need to analyze the emotion or try to understand where it comes from – a childhood trauma, a 'past' life, or a current story. Just be with the energy itself. The clarity and answers will come in retrospect, through your heart. In this way, you become the witness. You create space for your highest self to come to the forefront, the loving awareness of your soul. Your soul knows that all fear is an illusion.

And instead of getting pulled into the future or the past, you stay in the present moment… allowing yourself to access the core of this fear and feel how it makes you feel. And when you love yourself through it, it can move through your body and out.

You can clear energy in 30 seconds, although you may need to sit with bigger energies for a few hours or days. Some of your most deeply rooted wounds may take years to fully heal, as they will lighten over time.

You may wonder, *How can I truly clear the density from this lifetime and all others? Is it really possible to let this go in the span of a few months, a year, even a lifetime, when this has been my reality for eons?* But this journey is not about clearing one fear after another, one by one. It is energetic and multidimensional.

This process is happening exponentially faster than six months ago, one year ago, 10 years ago. It is happening every day, whether you sit with it consciously or not. You have already cleared astronomical entanglements of density within you. As the process continues to speed up, it is only inevitable that you will arrive at the point where everything is cleared. Someday, when you look back on it, you will feel immensely grateful and in awe of what you have done.

During my early to mid-twenties, I only cried once or twice a year. And I took pride in this. I told myself I was strong. Always 'happy.' I used my mind to control my perception of myself and how I was doing in life. I resisted and judged my sadness. I would see feeling sad or crying as a sign that I wasn't doing so well, or that my day was going badly.

Now I can see that I had put a steel wall around my heart. It was hard for me to feel my true emotions, so instead, I suppressed everything.

These days, I cry a lot – when I'm sad, happy, or moved. Instead of holding back, I let myself cry, allowing the emotion to pass through me. It doesn't make me strong or weak. And all of my emotions, all of my ways of being, are welcome.

When I cry with awareness, there is a part of me that is grateful – because it means I'm finally able to clear the suppressed emotions and energies I've been carrying. This is the deepest energetic work I can be doing. Through the tears, there's another part of me going, *Yes, it's happening. Let's let it all out.* I don't see it as a negative experience.

The days when you cry are good days, as you are clearing some big energies. Honor them, as this alchemy is necessary to come into wholeness. Whenever you let yourself feel your emotions with presence, or cry, or breathe them out, you are clearing a new layer, a new depth, of trapped emotion and energy. You are never repeating the same cycle. This is where the true energetic shift can happen.

Journal Prompts: Embracing Your Emotions

There may be certain emotions that you struggle most to feel, but in allowing yourself to feel them, you will find your greatest alchemy.

Ask yourself:

- What emotions do I resist or struggle to let myself feel the most? (For example, anger, grief, powerlessness.)
- Why do I resist feeling them?
- What emotions am I most uncomfortable seeing expressed by others?
- How do these emotions in others make me feel?

The next time you notice these particular emotions coming up (whether in you or in others), allow yourself to breathe deeply, telling yourself it is safe to feel them. Your most suppressed emotions hold the keys to the parts of yourself that you have been avoiding or rejecting. When you welcome them, you bring them back into the light. The more you sit with them, with compassion and awareness, the safer you will feel in your body when they come up.

All of this inner work allows the shadows to be illuminated. By releasing the dense energy, you are creating space in your cells to hold more light. Blissful light work, like sitting in meditation, allows you to tap into the light you have already anchored, remembered, and activated within you, and expand upon it. But it is the shadow work that brings in light where it is needed most. It is the shadow work you are doing now in your day-to-day life that anchors more light in your body and allows you to hold more of who you truly are, because you are releasing all that you are not.

Fluctuations in Frequency

Those of you who have been on this journey for a while may be noticing more peace and ease in your life. You have cleared many of your fears and they don't have the same grip on you anymore. Some will still rear their heads, but they will be more like echoes of the past. No matter how much inner work you've done, you may feel there's more clearing to do. This can feel exhausting and discouraging, but know that everything is accelerating.

It is normal for your frequency to fluctuate; in fact, it is an essential part of the ascension process. There will be days when you feel so peaceful, nothing can shake you... followed by days when you feel exhausted, vulnerable to the worries swirling in your head. And the contrast will feel like a loss: *I thought that calm was unshakable... but I'm back in my head again.* But you aren't going backward. You haven't lost anything.

When you're feeling peaceful in your heart and all your worries are far away... when you feel whole, trusting, and open... you are literally in a different frequency, experiencing another reality, another dimension, an expanded version of yourself. When your frequency dips, you start experiencing the denser thoughts and fears again. It is normal to notice more things in your reality that cause you stress. You may feel less stable in your ability to get back to the higher perspective and calm.

A misconception on this ascension journey is the idea that you should feel more blissful and 'high-vibe' all the time, and if you fall back into 'negative' situations, challenges, or emotions, you're not doing well.

But there's no such thing as falling back, and what you view as negative is simply your judgment of an event that is there for your highest expansion. It is a sign you are right on track. It is actually high-vibrational to sit with the heaviest emotions and let yourself feel them. The more you embrace this process, the more smoothly you will be able to navigate the fluctuations in energy, without being so attached to how you think you need to feel.

While you are continuously anchoring more bliss, peace, and trust, you are still in a phase of rapidly clearing all the density that you are holding on to. And so, you may feel like you are in a pressure cooker of one thing after another coming up for you to see and feel. This is a good thing — even though it can feel intense.

You are shifting your consciousness, and body, more rapidly than ever before. You are clearing dense energies not only from your own consciousness, but from the entire collective consciousness of humanity. Layer by layer, you are building an unshakable foundation of all the light that you are. Your daily life experiences, especially your challenges, are perfectly designed to allow you to see and feel whatever you need to clear. And when you're ready, you can choose a new way. A new response. A new possibility.

∞

Once you have healed many of your deepest wounds, you will start noticing the more subtle layers of density in your being — the ingrained fears that have always been running in the background, the beliefs that feel like facts, the patterns and habits that have been draining you energetically, even though you barely noticed them before.

When you have done a lot of healing, the remaining layers of density in you will feel like heavy weights. You are aware of them, you want them to go away, but they've been a part of you for so long... they feel impossible to move.

There may be times when you feel energetically drained and think you just need more rest, but what you really need is to face the emotions and disempowering stories you have been suppressing. But you'll find that it won't take as much time as before to sit with the emotion and let it go. Sometimes, being with your feelings, with full presence, is the greatest meditation you can do.

Nothing can be hidden from you anymore, and if it is, your body will get your attention. As you anchor more light, even the tiniest dip into density will feel noticeable. But even the lows will be higher than your highest highs in the past. This is still a linear way of explaining it. In truth, there is no hierarchy. It is all energy, and all of it is welcome. You are constantly expanding, no matter how you feel.

You are healing yourself every time you feel your pain and sit with it.

You are rising every time you choose to be gentle with yourself.

And you are ascending every time you open your heart with love.

Walking this journey is the most important thing you can do, because it affects how you feel, how you show up, and all that you experience in your life. It changes you, as it changes your entire reality. If you look back, you will see that there are things that you have healed at the core that will never affect you the same way again. You are trusting life more than ever before. When something unexpected happens, you will easily see it from a higher perspective, knowing that even your challenges are there for your highest expansion – as they always have been.

You are freeing yourself from the shackles of the past, moving through life with ease and creating from a fresh slate.

∞

When you see your shadow and the perfection of it all, you will know that you don't have to shun it or make it wrong; there is nothing to reject, suppress, or fear. You will start to have compassion for this part of yourself – this part that has felt so far from the light.

You will illuminate it with your heart's love, casting a bright light into the depths of yourself… And then, you can hold hands with your shadow and walk it back home to the light. As you do this, even the densest realms of this dimension will become more illuminated.

And as you find unification within yourself, you will see all of humanity unifying as one.

This is your process. You are doing it. And it's okay if it feels massive – because it is. Harmonizing the deepest shadows of your consciousness, across all existences…

This is what brings the weight of the entire world back to love.

This is what brings more light into the entire quantum field.

This is what it takes.

CHAPTER 7

Walking Between Worlds

As you are clearing the density in your being, you are creating more space to embody the light of your soul. You are shedding so much – not only your fears and suppressed emotions, but entire identities, priorities, and ways of being. In this transition, it is normal to experience a pause, a limbo space, between who you were and who you are becoming. This chapter explores what happens during this limbo space and how to navigate it smoothly.

You are quite literally walking between worlds: one, which you can see existing all around you, and another, which you cannot yet see, but can feel in your heart.

They could not be more opposite. The world you see is one of lack, division, and uncertainty. Society reflects this world, with its fear-based programming. The media reinforces this world, making everything look like it's getting worse. The world you feel in your heart is one of love, freedom, and peace for all. It is awakening, and things are getting better. It only appears to be getting worse as the darkness of the past is being purged.

The world you can see is crumbling before your eyes. The New Earth is emerging from the rubble. You have been jumping between the two realities every day, and this takes an immense amount of energy. And it has been hard at times to continue believing in the world you envision while everything around you seems the opposite.

You are the bridge between worlds. You are the living, breathing evidence of the new.

The key to the most beautiful world you can envision is in your heart. This is why you must trust the vision of your heart.

∞

As you raise your frequency, you will become more sensitive to the energies of the world you see that are not in resonance with your own. This is why you may crave more time alone or in nature. It feels exhausting to be around people with whom you cannot be your true, unfiltered self. You might find yourself drifting away from friends who don't resonate with who you are becoming, while keeping the true friends who love and accept you as you are.

Everything in your life that is not in alignment with your soul and assisting in your expansion feels suffocating, and this is why many people change jobs, entire careers, residences, and relationships at some point in their awakening journey. You may even feel you're walking in a dream, or waking up in a completely different world, unable to explain what you're going through to friends and family.

But navigating the shift between the old and new worlds out there is not the only challenge. It is your inner world that is changing most. You are navigating multiple deaths of old identities and attachments... changes in how you feel, think, and see life. This is why it feels like you're being squeezed from all sides. Fear and doubt can come up louder than ever before, because you're stepping into the complete unknown. You may also feel unmotivated, stuck, physically exhausted, and unable to think and function the way you're used to.

When you resist the changes, that's when you teeter-totter between the old and the new... unable to go back to the old, but afraid of the new. And this happens to everyone. It's part of the process. It takes time to fully release deeply ingrained patterns.

Embrace this phase between the old and new. You can call it 'the limbo space,' because this is how it feels. But you're not really in limbo, you're in a space of rapid transformation – like a chrysalis, where a caterpillar has yet to discover its wings.

This space exists to allow the old realities to fully dissolve and crumble, so that the new can come in. It reconfigures your outer reality so it can shift to match the frequency you have anchored within.

The Limbo Space

The limbo space allows you to let go of what you're ready to let go of, at your own pace. Many feel stuck in this place, yearning for what's next but not sure what to do. You may question your path. You may judge yourself, especially when you're not 'making progress' in the ways you're used to.

Most people start thrashing around here, reaching for something to cling on to. This creates more noise, fear, and self-doubt. The harder you try, the more roadblocks you run into, and you're left drained and defeated. You may no longer feel the same about something that once excited you. Or you may feel like any clarity you had about your path is fading into confusion.

When you notice you're in this space, it is counterintuitive, but better, to breathe into it... embrace it, and let yourself rest there. Allow yourself to be carried with the tide, instead of fighting it. You are not going backward. You are being recalibrated to make way for something new. And it is okay if it's a little quieter in the in-between space while the dust settles.

This is not a place for planning, controlling, or trying to force what's next. It is an energetic space, and much reconfiguring is happening here, especially when it looks like nothing is happening.

How to support yourself in the limbo space:

~ Know that nothing is wrong; you are right on track.
~ Practice being gentle and compassionate with yourself.
~ Ask your body what it needs.
~ Lean into the discomfort of doing less and just being.
~ Spend more time in nature, without devices or distractions.
~ Let yourself create or play just for fun, with no end goal.
~ Try to build spaciousness into your schedule and let go of any unnecessary obligations.
~ Allow yourself to sit with every emotion that comes up.
~ Validate and value your inner shifts, reflecting on how far you've come.
~ Let yourself dream big for fun, without thinking about the 'how' or next steps.

Your mind will look for evidence of physical progress and think nothing is happening. This is because it doesn't know how to sense and value the energetic subtleties of all that is recalibrating within. And you cannot measure your progress with the same measuring stick you have used your entire life.

Your greatest progress now is not physical – it is energetic. It is in the shifts in your frequency, which impact the dimension you experience, the energy you create from. It is in the clearing that is taking place in the deepest layers of your being, the amount of light that is flooding in, the opening of your heart. It is from here that you can jump to brand-new realities, leaving everything behind that doesn't align with who you are becoming.

Sometimes, you must slow down into stillness to receive what is next.

You may not look like you are doing a lot in the outer world, but you are moving mountains in your inner world. In fact, in the gap between shedding the old and stepping into the new, there will be many times when you think you are being lazy. This is because your mind will be telling you to do more, hustle, and figure things out, even while your heart is saying, 'That feels exhausting, and I don't want to do it that way anymore.'

It may feel like you're being lazy, because to move forward, you need to let go of the programming of rushing and hustling to feel you're doing enough… This is being dissolved, because your soul wants you to see that you are whole and complete, right here and now. You are everything, and you have everything you need.

Only once you feel this can you move from this space. But the energy with which you then do what inspires you or what needs to be done will be different. It will no longer come from lack, fear, or self-judgment. It will come from relaxation. Trust. Connectedness. And joy.

Of course, there's a timeline where you force your way forward, overthinking and overdoing. There's a timeline where you feel stuck and judge yourself. There's a timeline where you open up to ease and trust, and everything flows. And every possibility in between.

But trying to plan what's next in your head will feel tedious, because your greatest creations are not created in the mind. And the frequency of what you're calling in is so much bigger than anything you can conceptualize.

Your soul is trying to show you there is a better way.

We'll delve into a new way of manifesting in Chapter 11, but in the meantime, here is a reframe: Maybe you're not being lazy; maybe you're just tuning in to the pause your soul is asking for in this moment. Maybe this pause is helping you avoid another detour, another distraction, that your mind wants to pull you toward. Maybe this pause is the recalibration you need to align yourself with the rhythm of your soul. Maybe this is the season that ends up changing the course of your life.

In fact, this pause is absolutely necessary, and it cannot be avoided. It is the only place you can learn to sit with yourself in order to learn to fully be. Without this, you will never know the full light of your being.

This is the pause that breaks the autopilot cycle of doing. This is the catalyst for unraveling years of conditioning that pushed you to be productive, to achieve, to prove yourself.

> *This is the sacred hush that shines a spotlight on your restless mind until it finally quietens… giving way to the voice of your heart.*

In the pause, you break free from the timeline that no longer serves you… making room for a higher timeline of trust and ease to anchor. You are slowing down to open to the magic of what can come in when you let go.

At first, this is an extremely uncomfortable place to be, because your mind will fight you. There is great alchemy available to you here, especially when you allow yourself to squirm in the discomfort. Know that the pause can feel peaceful if you allow yourself to embrace it instead of resist it. As you pause, you are learning to love the version of you that will be ready to receive what is next. You are learning to love yourself as you are – without having to do anything to be worthy of it.

When it feels like you aren't doing enough and nothing is happening fast enough, this is precisely when you need to let yourself slow down and rest. Most people underestimate the amount of rest and recalibration needed when doing the inner work. Taking the leap of faith, facing your fears, feeling your feelings, listening to your heart – all of this takes an enormous amount of energy. But because it doesn't come with a flashing badge or outer validation, you don't put much weight on it. And you underestimate the exhaustion of facing yourself day after day and riding the seesaw between your comfort zone and your dreams.

In the stillness, your thoughts and fears, hopes and dreams, doubts and worries are louder than ever before. Facing the noise of this internal inferno is exhausting. It is exhausting because no one else can be there with you, no one else can do it for you – you must face it on your own. There is no hiding from yourself anymore.

So, you need deep rest… Not the rest of distractions and numbing, but the truly soul-rejuvenating rest of just allowing yourself to be… and loving yourself, just as you are.

It is human to reach for distractions to avoid having to feel discomfort, and everyone does this. Be gentle with yourself when you notice yourself doing it. With time and awareness, the distractions begin to feel more draining than the choice to let them go.

∞

For me, the limbo space was particularly challenging until I learned how to relax into it. During the two years of remotely consulting for tech companies after I left my full-time job in Silicon Valley, I refined my services so that I only took on projects that felt meaningful and clients that were aligned with me. My client work became more heart-centered, working with passionate founders and focusing on coaching and mindset as well as business strategy.

Even though this was mostly enjoyable, the message from my soul was clear: 'You need to stop working for the dreams of others and go all-in on your soul.' And so, I slowly wound down all of my clients until I was only working with one. It was a gradual process of winding down my hours and responsibilities, swinging the pendulum to put more energy into my writing and art. This slow weaning worked well for me, because it gave me time to build confidence in the direction my soul was nudging me in.

Still, it took me many long months to drum up the courage to part ways with my final client (and only income source). The discomfort of anticipating this terrifying yet inevitable step became unbearable, to the point where one day I put in my notice and finally quit.

The emotional and energetic relief was immediate. It felt like I had cut an invisible cord and released myself from the energy field of my client as well as the noise and pace of the technology industry. I was free.

There was no one to answer to now, no one to blame, but myself. I had taken a massive leap of faith, with no safety net to catch me, and no evidence of what was on the other side. I had already eaten into a large chunk of my savings, so I liquidated my 401K (retirement savings) to give myself some buffer room and invested a little in crypto.

Standing in the complete unknown, I began to thrash in the whirlwind of my doubts and fears. It was an excruciating internal battle. I felt stuck in a never-ending loop between 'Can I do it?' and 'I can't do it.'

My knee-jerk reaction was to dive back into productivity, brainstorming what to create or offer so that I could make money, but I resisted this urge with everything I had. I knew that I had to make myself sit in the absolute discomfort of 'doing nothing,' feel my greatest fears, and learn to love myself as I was. I had to slow down enough to unlearn the incessant need to be productive, to deprogram the belief that I needed to do more to be good enough. Whenever the fears came up, I had to sit with my lack and limiting beliefs around money.

For the first time in decades, I had no projects and no plan. (Writing and journaling didn't count, because I would be doing that anyway for fun.) I felt guilty for having so much free time in my days to do whatever I wanted, to the point where I couldn't fully enjoy them. And I realized that I'd internalized this guilt because of the societal programming that tells us we need to work a certain number of hours a day, or be consistently working hard and show up in a certain way, to be enough.

I spent what felt like endless dark nights fighting myself, seesawing between excitement and fear, stuck in the fetal position in the void of not knowing whether I could trust myself to take a step forward. It was a time when the whispers of my heart, urging me to keep going, seemed almost as scary as the multi-faced beast of fear that told me, 'Stay small. Stay safe. You can't do it.' The hopes of my heart scared me just as much as the fear of staying stuck.

My mind tried to rationalize this phase by telling me that the most productive thing I could be doing was learning to love myself when I wasn't being productive. The life that I wanted was on the other side of learning to let go and trust.

It took a couple months for me to relax my nervous system and loosen my grip on my old thought patterns. It wasn't a linear journey, because often I'd spiral into doubt again and feel like I'd gone 100 steps backward. But there were many more days when I let myself enjoy the spaciousness, get curious, and heed the nudges within. I kept writing and sharing on social media whenever I felt inspired, sometimes once a week or every few days. I took my journal to different artsy cafés and went for long walks to shake up the routine.

One day I was sitting in meditation and the vision for my first book suddenly came to me, with a rush of tears and warmth blooming in my heart as I imagined my future children holding it in their hands.

'This is my heart, this is my soul, this is my wish for you... and my wish for the world,' I would tell them.

The essence of the book came through with such a strong wave of love that it just had to be created exactly the way I saw it. I knew that it would hold not only my words, but my own paintings in full color... and every page, every brushstroke, would carry my love. I imagined this love rippling across the world, across generations of time and space... and perhaps, across the multiverse, as if it was a declaration from humanity to the universe: 'We are here. And we remember.'

The feeling of love and excitement in my vision was strong enough to catalyze me into action, and I began writing *Awakening the Heart of Humanity*, which I would self-publish the following year. And just as in my vision, it is a hardcover, written and painted with love.

Without a doubt, I know that if my mind had tried to come up with an idea for a book from the old restless energy, it would not have turned out the way it did. It would likely have been a self-help book written from the mind, not a book channeled from the heart... because who's going to buy a shorter, more expensive hardcover with my artwork as well as words?

But my vision came from the purest place of my heart, and it was never created to fit what I thought would sell well. I wrote it, first and foremost, for myself and for my future children – for the joy of holding a physical representation of my soul, captured in form. And at the same time, deep down, I knew that if it was meant to, it would fly with wings of its own and reach all the hearts who were calling it in. And it did.

I began to see that following your heart's excitement was the surest path to who you truly were – and who you wanted to be. The more

I let go of the noise of everything I thought I should do and instead trusted the unique expression of my heart, the more my writing began to shine… ideas began to flow… my online audience began to explode exponentially… and I stepped into creating, and selling, offerings that my old self could never have imagined me doing.

As my story shows, the limbo space is one of the most important phases of the process – between the death of the old self and the birth of the new. It is necessary, it is valid, it has meaning. And it cannot be skipped. Though it feels like everything is crumbling, this is happening for your rebirth. There is no way you can get it wrong.

> ***Let go, be curious, and let yourself be shown the way. The next version of you is already emerging.***

Trusting yourself, trusting life, means trusting that everything you are feeling, everything you are experiencing – including the lack of motivation or inspiration – is *exactly* what you need to be experiencing. It is for your highest expansion. It is a sign of your expanding consciousness.

Maybe you don't need to do anything to fix what's happening, because there's nothing wrong with where you are. All you need to do is embrace it and relax into it, knowing it's happening for a reason, knowing it is happening for you.

The void is temporary. Trust it will shift. Seasons of stillness shift into seasons of momentum. Some seasons last longer than others, but not a day longer than they are meant to last.

Listening to your heart means truly listening to its whisper… not what you think it wants, but what it's asking for. And instead of second-guessing the first hunch, instead of judging it or thinking it's not enough, trust it. Sometimes your heart will tell you to act. But often it will tell you to slow down and be gentle with yourself until inspiration naturally moves you.

Remember to trust and follow the tiniest nudges of excitement, no matter how seemingly insignificant, as we explored in Chapter 4.

Your consciousness is shifting, and instead of needing to be productive to feel fulfilled, you are wondering if there is another way. Maybe it doesn't have to be hard. Maybe you can allow and receive all the magic that you are.

This is the leap of faith within the leap of faith: letting go of the habit of forcing your way forward to open to the path of ease.

Have you ever wondered how easy it could be? How it would feel to trust the magic of the universe? Imagine finding yourself in the space of total trust and flow, breathless at the sight of your wildest dreams coming to meet you before you speak their name.

The path of ease exists. And it begins to open up for you when you relax your nervous system, your restless doing, and trust the natural movement of your body – whether it is called to rest, to nature, to music, to dreaming.

Trust the natural flow of your being. And trust this moment in your life, however it looks and feels, because it is giving you the key to it all. It'll show you the way, if you'll only stop questioning it.

Even when you think you are going backward, you are expanding.

Even on your lowest days, you are rising.

Every experience is leading you exactly where you're meant to be.

A LETTER FROM YOUR SOUL

Dear sweet soul,

I see you. You have been fighting yourself over and over again – and it feels like the battle will never end. Your fears and doubts are grabbing you by the throat, pulling you down, and you can barely gasp for air. This is an exhaustion unlike any other – the all-consuming exhaustion of being dragged down by your paralyzing fears, while wanting so desperately to trust your heart and take a step forward.

You wonder what you truly have to offer the world and whether what you're doing is any good. You see others who are shining and think they can do it better than you. And every day you wonder if you're just wasting your time.

Let yourself feel the full force of your fears. Hold yourself through the waves of doubt and vulnerability with compassion. They must be felt to be purged. Know that the heaviest days are a gift, because they are when you're finding your strength. They are when you're choosing your light, despite your fears.

And then, make it your daily focus to be fully yourself. Do it all your way. Don't get overwhelmed by the noise of comparison or try to imitate others. Your only task is to be fully yourself... because no one else can replicate your light. No one can do it better than you.

Ask yourself, 'What do I want? Who do I want to be? Is there a more fun way to do it?'

Ask yourself how you can make whatever you create a reflection of your heart, your essence. How can it be more you? How can you be more you? Follow the beat of your own heart, because this is your lifeline. This is your beacon in the dark. This is where you will find sanctuary from all the noise.

And it will be such a relief to be fully yourself. This is how you meet, and unleash, the full power of your soul.

You have your infinite heart, your gifts, and lifetimes of wisdom backing you. When you begin to trust this, you will uncover the most sparkling gems hidden in you – the sheer beauty of your unique frequency, pouring into everything you touch.

With love,
Your soul

Continuously Rebirthing Yourself

On this journey, you will experience multiple deaths and rebirths, with multiple limbo spaces in between each. The more you embrace them, the easier and quicker they will be.

As a human, you find comfort in defining and knowing who you are. When you embrace a role or identity in the world, whether it's a career path or a personality trait, you cling to it because it gives you a place to belong in this world. You get comfortable in that place.

As a soul, you like to explore all that you are – to go beyond labels and break free of attachments. The truth of who you are is beyond any human concept. Beyond any stereotype. Beyond thought.

When you open up to exploring all that you are in the most expansive sense of that phrase, you realize that this reality is not fixed – and you are not fixed. So, you must get comfortable with shedding your skins continuously. Just because you shed one identity and find a new footing in the next version of yourself doesn't mean it's going to stay that way. Sometimes within weeks or months, you'll find yourself shedding even that skin.

This is a journey of constant expansion. And the soul doesn't want to stay in one place, the soul wants to keep expanding.

Of course, you'll always keep the core essence of yourself. As you expand, you'll simultaneously go deeper into who you truly are. You'll let go of more foundational beliefs that you've held as fact. As you do this, your consciousness will shift, your entire being will shift. And inevitably, you'll continue letting go of all that you cannot take with you.

This shedding will look unique to everyone. It might not mean you are continuously changing what you do outwardly in the world. It isn't primarily about what you do, although this is one of many things you may feel called to change. It's more about the inner shifts – why you do certain things, the intention behind them.

For example, are you doing anything out of lack or fear? You may have taken a leap of faith to pursue a passion or create something that excites your soul, but are you hustling because you feel like if you don't, you'll fall behind? If so, even if you've stepped into something new, you're bringing the old energy and patterning into it. The lack and fear will keep coming up, until you can alchemize them so that you can show up in a more empowered frequency.

Your frequency is shifting exponentially. The amount of light anchoring on Earth is accelerating rapidly, hand in hand with your expansion. You will notice both subtle and major shifts in your thoughts, attachments, preferences, priorities, how you feel in your body, and more.

You may find yourself unrecognizable from who you were five years ago, or even one year ago. And eventually you'll find yourself unrecognizable from who you were a week ago. What felt aligned and in resonance a week ago might not feel the same now. And this is okay. Every day, you are new.

It's normal to feel disoriented by this speed of change. Embrace this journey. Become curious about the sensations rumbling in your being and what is wanting to come through you. Become an explorer of your inner world and discover what is being revealed to you.

Be okay with letting go of what once felt comfortable. If you notice fear coming up around that, breathe into it and sit with it. It's an opportunity to let go of another layer of fear.

Trust that you are on your highest path.
There's no wrong step you can take.

Let go of trying to control or resist the flow of life moving through you. You will begin surfing the waves. You will become the entire ocean, and more…

Anchoring into the New

Eventually, you will be able to walk between worlds, or shift realities, with ease. You will have anchored the higher frequencies within yourself and be able to hold your frequency steady wherever you go… whatever task you are doing, whoever you are talking to, no matter what is happening out there.

Instead of having one foot in the old, one foot in the new, and seesawing between both, you will be solidly anchored in the new. As the two worlds split further apart, the old will feel like a distant memory. Day by day, you'll be changing to the point where you no longer act, think, or live the way you used to.

In the past, you had to try hard to let go of the old. Now, you have let most of it go – and that is a massive shift. There is a big difference in frequency between thinking about the changes you want to make and actually embodying them. But here, you may feel disoriented by how different you feel. You may think, *What's wrong with me?* You may feel less motivated, less attached to the things that used to excite your soul.

What changed?

Perhaps the world out there did shift. But most of all, you changed. You began to trust your path and take steps toward your heart. You fed the new, instead of the old. Now, the old does not command your attention (or your fear) like it used to. You are not emotionally invested in it.

This is changing the way you feel, the reason you do things, the way you navigate the world. It can feel a bit strange. What you have known for your entire life… for lifetimes… is no longer the same.

There's a blank slate. Is this normal?

There is no normal anymore, for you have entered uncharted territory. Normal is an illusion of the past.

And it is not what your soul wants to experience anymore. You are ready for something new.

That something new is your own creation, your own exploration into all that you are, and all that you wish to be.

You may find yourself in a life that was a faraway dream for your old self. Perhaps you have created and experienced things that seemed impossible to the old you. But perhaps you still find that you can't enjoy the fullness of it, because the final cobwebs of your programming cast a shadow on what is otherwise so bright.

You are in another limbo space, a gap between how you feel and how you want to feel. Your frequency has shifted, but you're still living in the mind of the past. The doubts and fears may not be as suffocating as before, but they are still buzzing underneath, and perhaps more noticeable to you now that you are more aware.

Because of the density in this realm, it takes time for the reality out there to 'catch up' with the reality you have anchored energetically within you. But when you trust the vision of your heart more than the reality around you (and the lack that you perceive), you speed up the materialization of the next expansive reality. When you are grateful for where you are now, you are more at peace with life as it is – and this also collapses the gap between how you feel now and how you wish to feel.

Look within, and you will see how far you have come. You are less quick to anger, less quick to judge. And this is because you have journeyed into the depths of your own wounding and loved yourself back to life. You are quicker to trust, laugh, and cry without resistance. Quicker to not be so serious about it all. And this is lighting you up from the inside out. You can breathe more easily now.

Are you looking for evidence of the new world?

Look inside yourself. It is there. And in every moment, it is emerging.

VISIONS FOR THE NEW EARTH

I see people laughing, dancing, and singing in nature... There is an air of celebration, a feeling of triumph. 'We did it!'

Children are running around, barefoot on the grass. People are relaxing on rugs around the fire, connecting heart to heart, swaying to the music echoing softly through the trees. Everything is vibrant, shimmering. The stars, even the mountain flowers, seem to be glowing in celebration.

We catch each other's eyes throughout the night, acknowledging each other and this moment... knowing that this is the moment we have been envisioning and anchoring for years. There is no doubt now. We have arrived.

We. Did. It.

Anything is possible here. This is an existence of pure presence.

Trust every moment to be complete and give you everything you need… without needing to pull in a future moment or worry about the past. Trust this moment is whole, complete, and multidimensional.

There is no limitation in the present moment. You have access to infinite timelines, realities, and possibilities. And it is magical.

All you need to do is receive life, moment by moment. Trust your inner guidance and heart. Choose to let it be easy. Follow your whims and joys. And be the love that you are.

There is no need to worry here. Part of you is noticing the things that you think you should worry about. But there is a calmness underneath, and you wonder, *Should I actually be worried about this? Or is it just an echo of the past, a habit, an old fear?*

Why do you need to worry, when everything is unfolding for your highest expansion? It is unfolding according to your heart's vision, your intention, your soul's knowing. You are the one steering the ship. Not just your human self, but all of you – your soul, your higher self, your universe.

> ***It is all perfect. And you are safe.***
> ***You are held. You are loved.***

Where you are heading is even better, and more delicious, than your wildest dreams. Your embodiment of this is unlocking quickly now, as you remember who you are. This is a place you have been yearning to experience for years. For lifetimes.

You are here.

CHAPTER 8

Transcending Your Programming

Throughout this book, we have explored how your ingrained thoughts and patterns lock you into a certain frequency from which you create your reality. But expanding beyond the old is not just about letting go of the belief systems that no longer serve you. It is about completely shedding the mind that tries to control and analyze your way through life.

This chapter is dedicated to letting go of the mind, because your mind holds the most deeply rooted behaviors, patterns, and programs that keep you tied to a lower dimension. As you go deeper on this journey, you will see just how much your mind holds you back from how you want to be.

Letting go of the mind is an ancient concept, but it was only recently that I saw what it truly meant, and how essential it was for our ascension. It is not just about quietening the mind in meditation. It may be one of the greatest shifts you make, because it's about completely letting go of how you have lived until now… opening up to a brand-new way of living in the heart.

I have started seeing how much I rely on my mind to control, organize, and plan my life… to get ahead, stay on top of things, and protect myself from what could go wrong. So much mental energy goes into trying to control my life, from the big things like overthinking my career and preparing for pregnancy and motherhood, to the most mundane things like thinking about everything I want to get done and the never-ending chores around the house. Underneath this restless energy is a worry that if I drop some of the balls, I'll fall behind or things won't work out well. On top of this, more mental energy goes into judging myself if I feel I haven't got enough done.

In this ascension, we are all being called to take the leap into a level of trust that feels crazy to the analytical mind: knowing that everything is unfolding in perfect orchestration. And from the highest perspective, it is already done. Nothing that we do or don't do will take us off-course.

Can I trust this so deeply that I let go of the mind that needs to control my life? This means letting go of my perfectionism and overthinking, in ways that I have never done before. And this feels impossible, because my intellect and ability to figure things out have worked well for me; they have helped me create the life I have now. They are part of who I am. This is how I live. Over the course of my life, I have built and refined this way of being, and it has helped me feel safe, in control.

This is another choice point between the old and the new… the choice to take another leap into the unknown and realize a new level of being, held and supported by the universe.

I have asked myself, 'How am I supposed to let go of my natural instincts and do the opposite of what I normally do? If I let go, I feel like I'll crash and burn. For example, with my business, I naturally think about how it's going, what I should launch next, what I need to do more of… And all of this is both reinforced by the business-savvy world that applauds the hustle and warranted by my fears. If I let go, won't I lose all the progress I've made? Won't I disappoint my audience? How will I pay the bills?'

But underneath this hustle is a belief that I am not good enough, not there yet – an assumption that I need to control life because I do not yet have full trust in life, my soul, and my path. This is the old energy, and while this self-imposed pressure has pushed me to achieve beautiful things in my life, there is a more aligned way.

The new calls you to keep stretching your wings and rising, in the most uncomfortable ways. The old way was your comfort zone, but it cannot take you into your next expansion: into becoming the quantum field.

> ***You are being called to let go of the ways you control your life out of fear so that you can step into the higher frequency of faith.***

This is the leap into fully trusting you are everything… jumping off a cliff and landing in the arms of the universe – your universe, which is you. You unlock the next level of true impact, abundance, and flow when you dare to step into the opposite side of this energy… which is no longer trying so hard and trusting your frequency to bring in everything when you need it.

This may or may not drastically change what you do or create on the outside, but it will be a total shift in how you feel, what's behind the 'doing,' and how you experience life. Paradoxically, when you're in true flow and alignment with your soul, you will actually achieve more – but it will feel easeful and inspired.

Here's one pattern I've shifted. When I was feeling low about my work or comparing myself to others, I used to get on my laptop and start trying to be productive. But what I was actually doing was distracting myself from the emotions that needed to be felt. I started noticing the pattern, and whenever I felt the pressure, I let myself sit with the discomfort instead of ignoring it. Instead of giving myself the dopamine hit that productivity often gives me, I sat in the uneasiness of letting go, not needing to fix it or figure out a solution.

When you are willing to sit in the discomfort whenever it comes up, over and over again, you're clearing this energy of lack from your being. Slowly, I've loosened my grip on this pattern, learned to trust the flow of my life, my business – and most of all, love myself as I am, even when I feel low. Amazingly, this practice has healed a lifelong pattern of creating from pressure and force, giving me so much more energy to create when I'm genuinely inspired and moved by my soul.

The Programmed Mind

Before we go further, it's important to acknowledge the mind. The mind is an incredibly complex and beautiful part of you that allows you to function in this world and your body. This shift isn't about discarding the mind completely. 'Letting go of the mind' is about letting go of the denser patterns, habits, and addictions of the *programmed* mind – built over lifetimes of fear, survival, and conditioning.

This shift is about moving into harmony with the mind, so that you can come into the full embodiment of your mind, body, and soul. You are moving from the programmed and primal mind to the higher mind – or divine mind – which functions in complete presence and union with your heart and soul.

The higher mind is your super-consciousness – your connection to Source, your soul's wisdom, and all that you are, in this body and beyond. It has the ability to access everything you need to know, exactly when you need it. Instead of thinking in loops the way you are used to, when you're using your higher mind, you'll find that you simply call forth whatever you need to know. This is a life-changing shift into living in the infinite present moment, where everything opens up for you.

So much of this world has been built from the energy of survival, because this is the most primal part of the brain. Though the way the world looks has changed over the centuries, your base instincts have remained the same: to make sure you are safe, provide for yourself and your family, protect yourself, and anticipate what could happen. This shows up for people in different ways, but there is an underlying lack of trust in life – a fear that something bad could happen and take away your safety, your peace, your loved ones, or even your life.

It can feel like you are subject to the whim of forces that you believe are outside of you. You have tried your best to control whatever you can, but this has not eased your worries in a world that feels chaotic and often against you. And the whole foundation of this is based on the belief that you are separate from it all. From this perspective, at any point something can be taken from you.

In your current life, the number of actual threats you are faced with compared to your earliest ancestors is minuscule. And yet, you still operate from this primal brain, overloading your nervous system.

Your mind is very good at protecting you, but this holds you in a lower frequency of lack and fear – creating, and recreating, your reality from your beliefs. To create a world of freedom and abundance for all, where all beings know their divinity and just how supported they are, you must dismantle the entire survival paradigm, the most fundamental part of the brain.

You are ready to lovingly let go of this old programming. Your body and consciousness have shifted immensely, to the point where you don't need to live from the same survival energy as before. You don't need to keep recreating your reality from the lower frequencies.

*Now, you can create your reality from a
new frequency of trust, ease, and joy.*

There is a whole new reality available to you when you hold the frequency of oneness… knowing you are everything, you are absolutely safe, and you can walk through the world with ease.

Of course, you will still carry a healthy and rational amount of your primal survival instinct. If you are faced with an immediate threat to your life, you'll act instinctively. But even in this, you will be in full trust of the divine.

It is rare to find a human alive today who has ever tasted the fullness of living with no fear, in absolute connection with all that they are. And so, stepping into this brand new way of being is a monumental activation.

You are letting go of all the ways you think you need to use your mind to navigate life. Of course, you will use it; it will continue running in the background in a relaxed way. But as you let go of your fears and attachments, you'll begin living from the heart.

Letting Go of the Programmed Mind

How do you let go of the programmed mind? To be honest, I struggle with this, so please be gentle with yourself, too. Here's what I'm practicing...

Become aware of when you're in your head

First, when you're worrying, trying to figure things out, trying to control, overthinking the past or future, and so on, catch yourself. Let yourself feel the lack, worry, and pressure underneath. Every time you sit with the discomfort underneath, without trying to fix or resist it, you loosen its grip on you.

Recognizing when you're in your head is actually easier now, because it is becoming increasingly more draining to be in your head. What was once the norm now feels exhausting and heavy. The more you try to figure things out, the more your head hurts. And this is your body telling you to come into your heart and relax.

The more light you anchor in your body, the more you naturally get out of your head. Your frequency is so much higher than before. And so, when you're in your head, you feel the density of dipping back into an old pattern. You are more sensitive to the density, because it feels so out of place.

At first, as you bring awareness to your mind, it can feel as if your thoughts and worries are getting louder – but this is because the entire template of worry and control is coming up to be cleared. Be patient with this process, and keep observing yourself without judgment.

It also helps to be kind to your mind, instead of shunning it. It isn't your enemy; it's trying to protect you. Tell it: 'I see you. Thank you for watching out for me, but it's going to be okay. You can let go now.'

Come back to your heart

Second, choose to take a deep breath, come back to your heart, and lean into trusting the divine. The solution will come, the next step will come, but not when you're trying to figure it out. Let it go for now, surrender, and trust.

You may think, *It's easy for you to say, but my life is harder.* But this journey is hard and isolating for *everyone*, regardless of circumstances. Each soul's journey brings unique challenges and energies to overcome. And though all of our experiences are different, we must each feel, and alchemize, the entire density of the collective, and our ancestry, stored in our cells over lifetimes. It takes your entire being to be with yourself and watch yourself in every moment. Though the practice of witnessing and letting go of your mind sounds simple, showing up fully to it may be the biggest thing you will ever do.

When you are in fear, you are in your head. Come back to your heart. You cannot anchor a higher frequency from the head alone. The heart has an intelligence of its own. It draws you into the present moment, where everything is in absolute perfection, where you are expanding into the knowing that you are not a victim. You are not small. The more you play in this space, the more you will see this is how you access the quantum field and infinite intelligence that you are – through your heart.

Anytime you feel off-balance and caught in the loop of worrying, notice this is an old program. Bring your awareness to your heart, and make this connection your first priority. Sit in nature. Let the sun shine on your face. Bring yourself back to presence, back to this moment. There, you will feel the energy shift, your heart open, and a warmth bloom in your chest. And you will remember what you have forgotten: that you are divinely held.

Leaning into your divine connection is essential, because without it, you will keep looping in your head. When you are in your heart, you can feel your connection to it all. Nothing can hurt you, nothing can be against you, because you know you are an infinite soul. You are an eternal being of light. You know who you are and where you are heading, and you know there's nothing to fear.

At the thought of letting go of your usual defenses, your mind will scream and protest, 'But something bad will happen!' Your challenge is to keep letting go anyway – by leaning into your connection with Source, so that you can fully surrender and know you are held. Your soul, higher self, and universe have your back – 100 percent of the time.

You are letting go of all the ways you have tried to find security through overthinking, controlling, and doing. Your mind has helped you create a sense of security, but it has never been true security because you have always felt like you have to do more to stay afloat. True security is found in knowing, and trusting, your connection to it all – your inner being, your spirit, the entire universe.

This is where all fears crumble in the light of all that you are, because you will see with pure clarity that they are only illusions. They are only your programming speaking to you. They are not the truth, and you can let them go. Letting go does not mean disconnecting and not caring. Consciously letting go also means creating space to listen to the nudges of your soul and sitting with any emotions arising in you. If you're distracting yourself and feeling drained, you're not listening to your soul.

There will be days where you need to nap, take it slow, and be with yourself, when that's what your body and soul are asking you to do. When you feel exhausted or energetically zapped, that is a sign to let yourself rest and recharge – fully, without self-judgment. Trust that as your cup fills, you'll have moments of spontaneous inspiration – little nudges to do this, go here, do that… things you may not have planned for, but feel inspired to do. You'll open to true flow, which is not trying to overly plan or control your day, but allowing what you're meant to do to flow in and move you.

Acknowledge the moments that flow

The third step to letting go of the mind is to start noticing how well things flow when you're *not* in your head. When you're just going about your day, not really dwelling on anything in particular, all of a sudden inspiration may strike. An idea, an opportunity, a solution may come out of nowhere. This might happen when you're in the shower, washing dishes, or walking outside… Notice when this happens, because it's the flow of your universe moving through you, for you, when you get out of your own way. It's a synchronicity, a nudge from your soul. It's your universe providing you with what you need exactly when you need it, without you having to do the work to pull it in.

Of course, once inspiration strikes, you might feel like taking action on it. But this will feel easeful, because it's aligned, exciting, and synchronistic.

When you notice this happening more, you'll realize that when you get out of your own way, solutions still come. Things fall into place. What you need comes in, with less resistance. You don't have to work as hard to make it happen. You don't need to worry about it. Your challenges seem to resolve themselves.

When you live from the heart, you collapse time. An idea that may take your brain weeks to come up with can come to you in a split second from your soul. A project that would normally take you five hours to map out can be received in its entirety, like an energetic download, in 30 minutes of flow state. You melt into the present moment, slowing down within while everything outside of you speeds up.

You begin to flow with life, instead of thinking your way through it. But you can only trust that this is how it works by noticing and validating these experiences. This is the new way of being fully in the moment, receiving what comes in, and then taking inspired action.

Again, you aren't *discarding* your mind, you're letting go of the excess mental energy around overthinking and overexerting yourself. Thoughts will come, but there will be no attachment to them, no resistance – they will just flow through you. In this life, you've mastered what it's like to create from your mind. Now, it's time to open up to brand-new dimensions, the limitlessness of your soul.

This journey is about becoming fully present so that you can receive all of life. Most of all, give yourself permission to enjoy your life. If you knew that everything was unfolding with perfect timing, you would let yourself enjoy the present moment more.

The soul is not in a rush. When you fully open to this, it will feel like everything is rushing in and everything is speeding up, but your soul is always right on time.

The Perfectionism Template

One of the common templates, or programs, of the mind that you are being called to let go of is perfectionism. This is the perfectionism that comes from trying to control your reality, do more, strive for more, and worrying about the little things.

On this journey, you are naturally dissolving the perfectionism template as you begin to trust the divine perfection of it all. Instead of trying to be perfect, you are realizing you can just *be*.

The perfectionism template can show up as:

- mental addiction to overthinking, controlling, and planning
- the paralysis of procrastinating because you think you're not ready
- being hyper-critical of yourself and others
- dwelling on small mistakes and imperfections
- the fear of losing control, failing, and disappointing yourself and others
- wanting to be liked and seen in a certain way
- having high expectations of yourself

You are being called to shift from trying to control life through perfectionism to opening up to the perfect flow of the universe, the divine unfolding of everything.

> *There is no true perfection except for the perfection of this moment, exactly as it is, exactly as you are.*

Every moment unfolds the way it is meant to, including the imperfections that you perceive, to help you see yourself more clearly. If it doesn't go the way you want, that's a gift – something better is on the way. If you mess up, that's a gift – you can sit with the emotions triggered and let them go. Look at all the ways you judge yourself and hold yourself in separation from the divine flow of your life.

What if you don't need to worry about anything, big or small? What if you can fully trust that it is all working out for you, that you are guided, and that all those you love are guided too?

Even the idea that you need to be perfectly aligned, or perfectly ready, to receive what's next is keeping you from seeing how everything is already available and accessible to you. Every moment brings you exactly what you need to see. And if it were meant to be another way, you would experience it another way.

All of it is bringing you to love yourself more and dissolve yet another layer of separation keeping you from seeing the beauty of what is here right now… appreciating your unique essence and path, instead of comparing yourself to others or to where you want to be.

You can loosen the grip of perfectionism by telling yourself:

~ 'It is all unfolding perfectly, without me needing to make it perfect.'

~ 'It is always working out.'

~ 'I am where I'm meant to be.'

Some of these statements may be hard to believe, because they are being filtered through your doubts and old programming. But keep opening to them, and you will begin to notice how things flow when you get out of your own way.

When you tune in to your inner guidance, you will know what to do and what to say. You will complete everything that truly needs to get done. You don't need to police yourself anymore. Even if you miss something and make a mistake, that's okay.

When you stop worrying, you free yourself to think more clearly and hear the nudges of your soul, which allows life to flow more harmoniously. It is normal to feel unsure – you are brand new. Raw and open. Instead of hardening to this, keep softening. Soften into your heart. Let it hold you. And let it show you the way.

Changes in How You Think and Feel

You have already come so far. All of the inner work you have done has helped loosen and release the knots of density in your being.

Imagine your brain is like a giant knot of intertwining ropes, and all your beliefs, fears, past traumas, ideas, goals, and plans are individual knots that make up the big knot. The things you're most identified with, or attached to, are the most complex knots, as they're tightly wound and entangled with one another.

When you start loosening your attachment to your beliefs and fears, healing, and letting go of your traumas… when you start loving yourself and trusting life… even when you let go of the idea that you need to get somewhere, please others, or prove yourself… all these knots start loosening and unwinding. The mind has less to grab onto. It cannot keep running around in the same cycles.

And this creates *space*. You are no longer your thoughts. You are no longer operating from your patterning to react or protect yourself. You are no longer identified with who you thought you were.

You have fewer fears. Fewer plans. Fewer beliefs about how things have to happen. Less rigidity. And more peace.

You are able to allow others to walk their own path and have their own opinions.

You have visions and dreams, but you know you don't need to figure out how to make them happen. The highest plan feels like having no plan – and that is because you cannot plan anymore from your mind. When you try, it quickly exhausts you. Deep down, you know it will all come in, step by step, idea by idea, synchronicity by synchronicity, exactly when it is meant to.

You are shifting from trying to control and manipulate your life to receiving it moment by moment. Though ultimately this will bring you more flow in life, during the transition, rewiring your brain can feel incredibly uncomfortable. Your brain, and how you use it, is going to feel different as you move from thought to inner knowing, limitation to limitlessness, linear to infinite. You have never experienced your brain this way.

You won't be able to drum up the same worries and fears, and this will make you wonder if perhaps you don't care as much as you used to. But it's not that you care less. You are less worried – and in the past, worrying made you feel like you cared.

You'll notice more pauses between your thoughts, and this can feel disorienting at first. Until you get used to it, this newfound spaciness may not feel peaceful. It can feel more like a high-pitched buzz. Fewer thoughts, just frequency. It can feel like your brain is receiving and streaming energy without the words to understand what the downloads mean. It can feel overwhelming and electrical at times, and at others, exhausting and blurry.

If you feel uncomfortable in your physical body, know that you are adjusting to and assimilating ridiculously high frequencies that you are not used to.

Anchoring the Light

It's important to stop trying to function the way you used to. You aren't supposed to stay the same. This may be hard, especially for those of you who have been perfectionists, over-achievers, living from the analytical mind… you will literally feel like you're becoming a brand-new person, because these patterns you once identified with will fade away.

You may wonder, *Am I losing my drive, my motivation?* But you aren't. All that you're shedding is your fears, attachments, and ways of being that do not serve you anymore. In the past, your fear motivated you to go to great lengths. This underlying drive is shifting into more relaxation, faith, and acceptance of yourself.

> ***You are letting go of the fear that you're not doing enough or you don't have enough. Trust the dissolving.***

The paradox is, when you let go, you embody more of the light that you are. Then you are able to create more powerfully, instantly, for the joy of it… because this is who you are. And your light can shine even more brightly when you get out of your own way.

Creating from a place of lack will never bring you the same fruits as tuning in to the knowing that you are a powerful creator, you are everything, and you have access to infinite abundance when you embody that frequency. There is nothing more valuable than existing in that frequency, because you feel more connected and in love with life than ever before.

This is a natural process. You don't have to try to speed it up. Simply allow yourself to ride the waves. It is a much simpler, freer existence, if you let go – and this is the next level of your expansion. A new momentum moves you. You can, and will, create beautiful things, but they will come from love, not fear. From inspiration deep within. Excitement to experience all that you are. And though you'll love creating, you'll also love just being. You'll know you don't have to do anything.

This is a brand-new freedom. It is the life of the soul, embodied. And this is a freedom that is your birthright. This is a freedom that is anchoring in every cell of your being. This is the freedom to truly let yourself receive life, be in life, and be fully yourself, right here and now.

∞

Who knew the courage it would take to choose trust over fear? Who knew the courage it would take to let yourself relax about something your mind said you should be worried about?

Who knew that it would actually be harder to teach your nervous system to rest than to tense up? Who knew it would take a great rebellion – against yourself and the entire world – to listen to the whispers of your heart telling you, 'You don't need to worry. It is all working out.'

It takes courage to resist the urge to try to figure things out when your mind keeps screaming at you to go faster. Leaning into trust feels absolutely crazy… and you won't be able to explain to anyone (even yourself) why you don't have a plan.

It can feel like you're splitting in two. Your body is actually more calm and relaxed than ever before. Your heart is softening, opening, trusting. But your mind sometimes gets stuck in the old thought loops and patterns.

You're between the old you and the new: your mind, stuck in the past, repeating the loops; your body, anchoring the new, feeling calm.

Your mind is just playing the role it knows best. But your heart knows truths your mind has not yet caught on to. Your heart knows it is safe to be relaxed.

Now, it's getting easier to trust your heart. Its calmness is replacing the worries of your mind. Trust is becoming your default state of being.

You are dissolving all separation...

CHAPTER 9

Dissolving Separation

We have spoken about how, in this physical incarnation, we exist in the illusion of separation. All of this inner work that you are doing, and have done, is clearing the density that you hold in your being... allowing you to come into union within yourself.

The full embodiment of this comes with letting go of the idea that anything is outside of you – that is, letting go of the entire concept of separation, which is held in place by the mind. In this chapter, we will explore how to transcend this separation.

Your entire life, you have believed there's you, and there's everyone else. There's you, and everything outside of you. You, and life happening to you.

This is how you have always experienced reality. And so it takes a mighty unraveling to let go of this illusion that feels like fact to you.

Nevertheless, you are dissolving the illusion of separation between matter, time, and space.

The Separation of Matter

One way you hold yourself in separation is believing you are separate from others, nature, the world, physical objects, and everything you see out there. This is the illusion of separation of matter. Instead of seeing everything as one energy, one consciousness – atoms and molecules all dancing together, vibrating at different frequencies – you view yourself as a human separate from the world. You view others as outside of you, the universe as outside of you, God as outside of you.

For example, a belief held in separation is, 'They are judging me.' When you believe others are separate from you, you can have the experience of feeling judged or comparing yourself to them. As you dissolve separation, you see others as aspects of yourself, reflections that you have created for yourself. The experience of feeling judged is happening for you because there is a part of you that is judging yourself, so that you can feel – and clear – your insecurities and come back to your heart.

The perspective of separation has served you in your experiences as a physical being, because it has allowed you to experience yourself as a fractal of the whole. And this lens has allowed you to experience physical reality, where you interact with, and learn from, your 'outer' world. But as you expand, you are going beyond all limitation to see that it was just an illusion.

The Separation of Time

Another way you hold yourself in separation is through the illusion of time. For example, the idea that, 'I'm not there yet,' the belief that you're behind or that you need to do more, is rooted in separation. You can shift this to: 'I am exactly where I'm meant to be.'

Time is a construct in this dimension, but, as you know, everything is happening now. Every timeline exists now; the past, present, and future are all happening now.

You may feel like your loved ones who have passed are gone forever, because you cannot see them anymore. But their energy is right here, and you can tap into it. You can still communicate with them. The timeline where they are alive and with you (which you perceive to be in your past) is also happening right now in the quantum field.

The future is also happening now. Your future self who is living your dreams, your ascended self, and the world you envision – they all exist now. It's just that in this dimension, you can only perceive the moment in front of your eyes. And in your mind, you hold memories of and attachments to the past, as well as hopes and fears for the future. Your mind creates the linear illusion of time.

If you imagine a horizontal line symbolizing time – the past, present, and future – you have been running along this line, rushing to get to the next thing. But the keys to the universe aren't found on this linear path. They are found when you stand still and let yourself dive into the depth of this moment. The moment you allow yourself to just be where you are, a portal will open up right where you are standing, expanding infinitely, touching all timelines and possibilities.

Everything exists in the depth of this moment. Go within your eternal being and you will find infinity in this moment. Your experience of time is already becoming more fluid, stretching, and quickening. It feels like time is speeding up or slowing down, becoming more fluid to show you that it doesn't really exist.

The Separation of Space

And third, you're dissolving the illusion of separation of space – the belief that there is an empty void of nothingness between two things. There is no corner of the multiverse that has absolutely nothing in it. In this quantum field, everything is energy, fluctuations of possibility. Everything is conscious. Physical objects, plants, and trees, may not appear conscious the way you see it, as a human. But they are conscious, because they are all you.

Everything that you see in your holographic reality exists because you are here to see it. To create it. To perceive it. There is no distance between things when it's all happening here and now.

∞

Space, time, and matter go hand in hand. As you dissolve the separation, you realize what your eyes see and what really is are worlds apart. You begin to let go of the mental limitations you've placed on this reality and open up to a brand-new way of perceiving the world.

This unlocks new abilities that may seem supernatural to your old self. For example, telepathy is becoming stronger for many around the world. Telepathy isn't technically about reading someone's mind, it's about tuning in to the same frequency as them and having the same thought or emotion at the same time.

People are already experiencing telepathy with those they love and are highly connected with. Twins, lovers, and best friends experience this, as well as parents with their children. Often, you finish each other's sentences or have the same 'random' thought at the same time. You know what the other person is thinking or feeling.

This is only just the beginning of true telepathy. You are realizing you are (all) one energetic being. And when you understand this, telepathy becomes quite ordinary. Because there is no separation, you are ultimately just communicating with yourself.

On the New Earth, it will become easier to communicate with everyone heart to heart, soul to soul, mind to mind. Telepathy will become the norm, as you will be able to pick up on and read another person's energy and intent as clearly as your own. All beings will become more connected to their hearts and one another, and this will pave the way to a world of harmony.

Even if there were to be any beings with malicious intents or ulterior motives, they would not be able to slip by unnoticed. People would see right through them. It will no longer be possible to control humanity through fear, manipulation, or the abuse of power. And this will allow a flood of new systems, leaders, and ideologies that truly serve humanity's highest good to triumph.

VISIONS FOR THE NEW EARTH

No words are needed. There is a shared understanding, and it is as if we are telepathic. We can feel each other; we can feel the love between us from any distance. It is palpable.

Even the wild animals – they aren't afraid of us. The fox comes closer, curious… and a little butterfly flutters by to say hello. We are one with nature, one with each other and with all living beings.

And life will never be the same again.

Letting Go of Seeking

Don't confuse this ascension journey with an endless pursuit to become something and reach something that does not yet exist within you. This path has never been about doing more and seeking more. It is about coming home to your heart, your connection to all that is, and living from this place of deep trust and love, in full mastery.

Living in full mastery isn't about activating your gifts, remembering past lives, or embodying the mastery you had in previous lifetimes. It's about knowing all that you are – now. You are Source, embodied – now.

To walk into your full mastery, you don't need to do anything to improve yourself, access your gifts, or strengthen your Source connection. These are human ideas that keep you in separation, endlessly seeking and thinking you're not there yet… thinking you need to do more, or be more, to get 'there.' But 'there' isn't a destination, it's simply the truth of who you are. To accept it, you must let go of seeking.

Seeking helped you get to where you are now. But the next expansion is about letting go of even that, because you are stepping into the full remembrance that you are already there. You have always been God. You walk in full mastery when you accept who you truly are – and then live from that place of knowing.

How do you stop seeking what you already are? Your soul will tell you, 'Know that you are already there.' But your human aspect will say, 'But how can I be there if I don't feel like I am?'

It can feel like you have a long way to go, because you're still seeking to feel good. You're still wanting something different from what you're experiencing now. You still have fears, habits, and reactions – things you want to improve or change. You still get in your head and you feel like you have further to go.

Shifting into embracing whatever you're experiencing, even when you're feeling low, allows you to start living in a new way that dissolves your resistance. Let go of judging where you're at and see the gift of the present moment.

Your body is integrating light so much faster now than ever before. On this ascension journey, everything is changing rapidly. What was true for you three months ago may not be true today. What worked for you five years ago may be what is holding you back today. It is now time to allow yourself to receive who you are *today*. Not who you were in the past, not the way you used to have to navigate life. It is time to see yourself with fresh eyes, anew.

Let go of trying to work hard on your journey, because it is already unfolding in absolute perfection. From the human perspective, it feels like it takes a lot of time to heal and shift, but from the highest perspective, it doesn't need to take a split second of your time. All you need to do is be here fully, and let go. And you don't even need to try to do that. Just be here.

> *It is time to receive all that you are –*
> *right now, in this moment.*

When you seek something that is not 'here,' you resist where you are now and who you are now. And in this, you miss all that you are – and all that is available to you right now. Remind yourself to live from moment to moment, seeing every moment as whole and complete, and opening up to a brand-new way of experiencing pure presence. There is so much vibrancy and aliveness here.

This is where the door opens to the infinite, a portal from you… to all of you. This is where you can finally meet yourself. This is where the light that you are shines without any dilution, any distortion. It is where everything exists. And nothing needs to be, because everything exists.

Your heart is being prepared to hold, and anchor, more love than ever before. You are releasing the barriers between your heart and all the love there is – and this is showing you that you *are* all the love there is.

All the love in the world, in the multiverse, across all dimensions… This is who you are.

Embracing the Flow of Abundance

One common example of seeking, rooted in lack, is feeling like you don't have enough money and seeing money as scarce. If you believe money is outside of you, separate from you, something you need to work hard to hold on to, of course it will feel limited.

Money is one form of abundance in this reality, but true abundance is fully trusting the infinite nature of your being, the infinite nature of a universe that is constantly giving to you and reflecting to you all that you are. And when you know this in your bones, you will see all of your experiences match this. You have everything you need when you need it. You live in total freedom – to be yourself, to dream big, to live as you like… the freedom to live without fear, the freedom to live in your heart.

True abundance is unlocked when you free yourself to embody all that you are. Embodying your light magnetizes everything to you.

It takes a leap of faith to lean into this knowing when your current reality reflects lack and urgency and your mind is spinning with thoughts like *How am I going to have enough?*

And this is why instead of trying to take the leap of faith through your mind, forcing your mind to believe in something it does not yet see, it is more effective to take the leap of faith through your heart.

Anchoring the Light Activation: Opening to the Flow of Abundance

Appreciation unlocks the flow of abundance. Appreciate yourself and this moment, without looking for what is missing. When you're outside and your nervous system feels a bit more relaxed, feel the calm presence of nature holding you, the sunshine on your face. Even when you're sitting at home, noticing the laundry that needs to be folded and all the things you need to do, take a deep breath and change the lens through which you see your life.

Look at it all through the eyes of appreciation. How grateful are you to have this home to care for? This warmth, this love in your heart, this life to create... the chirping birds and life-giving sun... on a planet where you can feel everything and be anything. How beautiful it is now, even in its mess. Know that your soul is choosing to experience all of it, exactly as it is.

Imagine yourself as the energy of abundance itself. This entire universe is yours, and it is constantly reflecting your frequency back to you. Keep coming back to this knowing, and choose to make it more real than all the lack you see out there. You must first tune yourself to the frequency of abundance within so that your reality can shift in response to you.

True abundance isn't about money. It is possible to be in debt and feel more abundant, connected, and divinely supported than a multi-millionaire who feels disconnected and lost. Open your heart to feel your connection with everything. This is how you tune in to the frequency of abundance within you and all around you.

The frequency of abundance can be felt differently, depending on the person, but it is the joy of being alive, being all that you are. It is feeling utterly safe, secure, and unshakable. It is a sense of unlimited creativity and possibility, feeling totally free to be and do anything you want. It is knowing that everything you want to experience is coming in. And whatever you need comes in exactly at the moment you need it – perhaps not necessarily when you want it, but always in perfect timing.

This opens up an entirely new way of experiencing life, where your old life of rushing, fearing, and living in lack is a distant memory. It will feel like another version of yourself, a lifetime ago.

Everything Exists Within

Another example of seeking is looking for guidance outside of yourself, thinking you don't have the answers. Like many, you may have spent much of your journey looking for signs from the universe, asking for answers, wanting validation. But when you look for something outside of yourself, you're giving your power away. You're not fully acknowledging that everything you seek is within – and you have the power to call it forward.

When you sit down to meditate or pray, sometimes you feel like you're waiting for a message, a burst of clarity. You may visualize your higher self, your guides, or Source as external figures – and this keeps you in separation.

> *Instead of seeking 'out there,'*
> *look within. Ask yourself, and trust*
> *that the answer will come.*

The answer is right there, at your fingertips. All it takes is a second to get out of your own head. Some people might require more time to get out of their head and stop thinking that they don't know what they're meant to be doing. But all you need to do is know that you have the answer within, and it will come. Dare to ask the question, and trust that the answer is coming.

The moment you get out of your own way, you will see that in your heart of hearts, you already know – and the more you practice listening, the more you will trust your inner knowing. This is no longer about receiving from the universe outside, but receiving from yourself as the quantum field. You are ready to see yourself as your universe, your higher self, Source, and the entire multiverse.

Even with practices like meditation and any rituals you do, ask yourself: 'Am I doing this because I think I need to connect with spirit?' These practices may be beautiful and help you come into presence, back to your heart, but remember, you are always connected, whether you do them or not. Let go of making them a chore, making them something you 'have' to do to connect. Let go of any guilt around skipping them. You are opening up to a new evolution, where you can do these practices and rituals for the joy of it, whenever you feel inspired, while knowing all of your life is sacred, all of your life is a living meditation, and you are always connected to spirit.

Right now, you are standing at the doorway to the full realization of all that you are. Holding on to separation and the methods that worked for you in the past are only delaying you from walking through that doorway and fully embracing, embodying, and recognizing the truth of your being.

You have spent this life feeling homesick for a place you couldn't name… but you have always been there. You have always been your own home – it's just that you have forgotten.

You are the love that you seek.

You are the light that you seek.

You are all of it, and more.

There is no destination, because your soul already exists where you're wanting to go. This journey isn't about getting somewhere – but about remembering that you never really left.

Make this fundamental shift, and it will change everything. Instead of waiting for something to happen, waiting for the universe to answer you, recognize your full power as the universe. Instead of waiting to feel ready, command your reality and start creating your life with more conviction and trust. Create the answer you're looking for. Call forth the knowing from within.

This is how you create the momentum, trust, and ease that you're yearning for. This will feel absolutely magical to you; it is a place of total empowerment. It will bring you so much joy to be completely in tune with the melody of the universe… and you will gain immense reverence for the incredible experience it is to live, to create, to experience life as you are.

Dissolving the Belief That You Are a Human

Even the most fundamental beliefs that you hold as fact are coming up now to be looked at through new eyes and dissolved – including the belief that you are a human. You are not *just* a human. That is only a tiny fractal of who you are. Your soul exists in infinite dimensions and realities all at once.

Letting go of the belief that you are a human feels absolutely crazy, because you have been a human for as long as you can remember, in this life and many others. Shifting from 'I am a human' to 'I am everything' is a tremendous leap. No being has fully gone there before, because in every existence and dimension there has been a level of separation, a level of identification with yourself and who you are in this life. But knowing you are everything dissolves all separation. This is the truth that changes everything. This is the portal that marks the 'before' and 'after' between your old self and the beginning of a brand-new way.

Everything changes when you realize you are so much more than you have believed yourself to be. You are not powerless. You are more powerful than your wildest dreams.

> *You are not just a human. You are a soul.*
>
> *You are not limited. You are limitless.*
>
> *You are not alone. You are everything.*

Until now, you have been living life conforming to the constructs and limitations of being a human. As you expand your consciousness and realize you are not just a human, the old constraints of your reality begin to bend and shatter. You see that all your limitations have been held in place by your consciousness, both individual and collective... by what you have believed to be true. And these limitations can be shattered just as easily by your consciousness, and they will be as you begin to tune in to who you truly are.

This isn't about discarding the beauty of the human experience or trying to escape being human. It's about remembering that you're not *just* a human experiencing a human life, you're a soul experiencing a human life. And you are Source experiencing consciousness and all that you are.

You came here to awaken to all that you truly are, while being a human. As you clear the density of many lifetimes, you bring the fullness of your light into this reality, this experience, onto this Earth. And so, as you let go of the idea that you are just a human, you will also let go of the idea that you are just an individual soul.

You might feel some grief as you step through this portal, as it is the ultimate death of all that you have identified with across all of your existences – the death of identifying as this soul. This can feel sad, because in so many lifetimes, you actually came to love who you were. You came to love your essence, energy, strengths, and quirks. You found comfort in who you were, so to be asked to let that go feels like a death.

But it is only the human perspective that makes you feel like you're losing something. When you step into the knowing of the Oneness that you truly are, you remember you are everything. You can hold all that you have ever been – all of your experiences, lifetimes, lessons, and gifts as a soul – as well as the frequency of being everything, the quantum field, and Source.

You can access it all anytime. You can access any experience. You can travel across time and space and revisit anything you wish to experience again. Will you choose to do that? Maybe not. But you can.

So, you won't be losing anything. But to walk through this doorway, you may need reassurance that all is not lost; you are not actually dying.

Anchoring the Light Activation:
Acknowledging How Far You Have Come

It is beautiful to acknowledge this rite of passage. Give yourself a moment to reflect and appreciate the beauty of your life experiences as a human, and soul, up to now... acknowledging how far you have come and everything you have gone through to be here now.

Take some time for yourself and put your hand on your heart. Witness yourself, with eyes of love, acknowledging how hard it has been, and the dark nights you have endured to find your light. Look back at your life and cherish the highs and lows of the human experience. See the gifts and challenges and everything you've learned. You deserve this acknowledgment. And it will bring a deeper readiness to see what's beyond the door of all that you have been.

You are the one walking yourself home. You are the one placing one foot in front of the other. You are the one with your hand on the doorknob, opening the door.

You have always been the one.

The Grief of Feeling Separate from Source

Perhaps the greatest grief your soul has experienced, in life after life, is the grief of feeling separate from Source when you incarnated and forgot who you were.

You were never separate from Source, but you truly believed you were because you felt so lost in the darkness.

In every lifetime, this was your first, and ultimate, experience of separation. At first, this grief might not feel tangible to you; it's not at the forefront of your conscious experience. But every soul holds this deep grief of feeling like you are losing yourself, over and over again.

In every lifetime where you forgot who you were, you were plunged into the extreme opposite of the light that you come from. It was the greatest grief for your soul to endure, and you carry this grief in your cells because it has been compounded by life after life of pain and loss.

This grief has been hidden underneath every sadness you have experienced in every life. Even if you do not remember this grief consciously, the next time you feel sad or lost for any reason, allow yourself to be with the energy of grief and look it in the eyes.

Let yourself meet it fully. Give it space to speak to you and be felt through you. As you allow it to reveal itself, you will touch the core of it. And with every tear, every deep breath, you will move it through your body and out, simply by shining the light of awareness on it.

Anchoring the Light Activation: Connecting with Source

As real as your disconnection has felt, you have never been separate from Source. (You can use whatever word you like for Source: 'God,' 'the universe,' 'Oneness,' etc.) So, open your heart to remembering your connection.

Close your eyes, and imagine the light in your heart spreading to touch everything within and around you. This is the brilliant light of Source.

Breathing deeply, imagine expanding your energy outward to become everything. Imagine yourself as Source, and visualize yourself as pure light. Play in this energy, and tune in to how exhilarating it feels to receive all that you are.

It is okay to wipe the slate clean and start with this as the truth of who you are – this feeling of oneness and joy. Trust this is more real than any fear, any separation that you ever felt was real.

Can you trust that what you feel when you're in your bliss is so much more real than lifetimes of illusion? That is the leap you are being asked to take… choosing this as your truth.

At first, it may feel fleeting, but to the soul, this bliss is more familiar than anything. This is the foundation you can lean on, whenever you feel wobbly in your trust. There is nothing at all to fear. You will not even fear death, because you will know that death is not an ending but a portal into all that you are.

The Fear of Death

Even though the fear of death might not be at the forefront for you every day, it is the core of all other fears. You have experienced death in countless ways across all of your lifetimes: your own traumatic, painful, or lonely deaths, grieving the deaths of your loved ones, or witnessing war, murder, and disease. And in some lifetimes, you have been the one who has taken another's life, because you have been it all.

To the human, death is an ending – the end of everything that you have known. It is the ultimate separation from life and loved ones. The final walk into aloneness.

To the soul, death is a gateway into all that you are. It is a shedding of your physical body, but your consciousness remains. Your awareness expands to experience all that you are as a soul in other realms and dimensions where you exist simultaneously. You see that this lifetime was happening alongside all of your other existences, including existing as Source.

Letting go of the visceral fear of death and the idea of separation is tremendous for the human who has no proof of what lies beyond death.

Anchoring the Light Activation: Letting Go of the Fear of Death

Just like with any other fear, you must first sit with the fear of death and feel it in your body before it can be let go.

In meditation, you can tune in to your body and set the intention to see where you hold the fear of death. You may notice a general sense of anxiety or tightening in your heart, pelvis or root, belly, throat, head, or perhaps everywhere in your body.

Let yourself breathe into this space, feeling into your fear of losing your loved ones, losing your life, and your heartbreak for all those who are suffering on your planet. You may feel the collective helplessness that this brings up, or the anger, frustration, and rage. And as you feel this, you may notice deeper energies coming up for you, like utter grief or existential dread.

You may find yourself journeying into the energy of the deaths you've experienced in other lifetimes or the deaths you've inflicted. It's important to let yourself simply be with this energy, without judging yourself or making up a story around it. Simply witness it. Breathe deeply, feeling compassion and love for yourself.

Imagine your energy expanding so much that you are the entire universe. See it all through the lens of the soul, and see the harmony and balance of it all. See how it has all been part of the divine experience of consciousness. See it without fear or judgment.

Only then will the energy start to shift, and you will begin to embody the knowing of the soul: *There is no separation. There's only you and more of you, consciousness and all of consciousness.*

There is no separation, but the idea of death as an ending has given humanity many gifts, including the gift of fully appreciating what it means to be alive, because at any second you believe it can be taken away from you. It has given you the primal urge to create meaning out of life and leave a legacy. Look at what humanity has created from this: music, art, books, the pursuit of knowledge, new tools and technologies, beautiful architecture, and so much more.

There's something extraordinary about human love – it shines brightly because of the contrast of the loss, grief, and death that you experience.

You love despite believing it can be ripped from you. You love despite all the darkness and loss. You choose to love fiercely in this blip of a lifetime, even though you believe it will end.

Unity Consciousness

As you dissolve separation, you anchor the frequency of Oneness: unity consciousness. You begin to see everything as one and your undeniable connection to it all. When you step into this, you won't lack for anything.

But you look at the world, and say, 'No one lives like this!'

Those who buy into the separation, which right now is the majority of your world, will of course experience a life of separation, because this is what they're creating. So, you will find evidence of a world of separation, struggle, and lack. But you are here now because you are courageous and willing to listen to the call of your soul and see if there is another way of being.

Despite how it may appear, humanity is not becoming more separate and divided. The entire world is going through a massive initiation into unity consciousness. This is why all the division in the world is being highlighted: the energy of division is coming up to be fully seen and purged.

You are seeing it more than ever before, and it feels like you are going through a global dark night of the soul… because you are. The more you collectively hold on to the ideas of separation and division, the more painful it will get… and this is why it must dissolve – because you cannot keep going the way you have been. Through the darkness, the dawn can break.

The over-identification with who you think you are in this life, paired with under-identification with your soul and the soul of humanity, causes the most separation, hate, and grief on your planet. As more around the world remember the Oneness that they are as a soul, the separation will dissolve.

When you see yourself as love, you see others as love. The illusions crumble, walls shatter... and all that is left is peace.

Peace on Earth is inevitable, because the expansion of human consciousness is inevitable. And it is happening now.

CHAPTER 10

Embodying Your Light

The shadow work you have been doing of feeling your emotions, clearing the density, and transcending limitation is so important, because this is what allows you to open your heart to your light. You have come so far, and you are now ready to lean into embodying your light.

What does it really mean to embody your light?

This is about remembering – knowing – you are already embodying it, because you are Source. But in terms of bringing it into your daily life experience, this is about unifying all aspects of your soul as one, unifying the shadow and light as one, and ultimately experiencing yourself as the Oneness that you are while in this physical form.

And yet, embodiment is not about what you do. It is about how you are being – who you are being when you fully accept, receive, and become the light that you are. This is a new frequency that ripples out onto the Earth to touch everything in your life, and everything you do or say. This is the frequency that elevates everything.

You have done the inner work. You have journeyed into the depths of your darkness. You have sat with the deepest pain. Your heart has broken with the cries of the Earth. And now, it is time to let yourself feel the fullness, the brilliance, of your light.

In a way, this may be harder to do than sitting in your shadow, because accepting your light brings up so much fear for the human. It feels like the complete unknown. It feels too good to be yours, too bright to hold.

Embracing your light takes as much courage as embracing your shadow, because in the world there are still billions more stuck in their shadow than dancing in their light. Those who dance in their light, who have already integrated and alchemized their shadow, stand out because they are few and far between. They're scattered across all corners of the Earth, but you don't encounter many in any particular area. And so, they stand out in their communities and amongst their friends.

It takes courage to let yourself hold the light, be seen, and see yourself as the light, because the consciousness of the planet hasn't been ready for this. There has been too much wounding, which gets triggered when people see the light that they do not yet see in themselves. There has been too much programming, which makes them think, *How dare you shine so brightly?* There has been too much suffering, so they say, 'How dare you feel joy when so much of the world is broken?'

The hands of millions upon millions have tried to pull down those dancing in the light, because the brilliance of this light is like a bright flashlight, making them see and feel what they aren't ready to see and feel in themselves. This light is like a mirror, and though it's reflecting their own light, they aren't ready to receive it, because they feel unworthy. The mirror makes them cringe in a way, because what they see is clouded by their own judgment of themselves. And they cannot bear to look at it.

And so, instead of seeing the light within, they scoff and say, 'How dare you shine so brightly when I feel so low?'

In countless lives, you were persecuted and beaten for being who you were. And this created a deep wound, etched in your cells… making you hide, wear masks, and shrink into the illusions of who you are not, just to avoid becoming an outcast again.

But this is the lifetime where you reclaim all the light that you are without fear, filter, or resistance. This is the lifetime where you find the courage to hold the light high like a brilliant beacon, allowing others to see that it is safe to hold theirs, too.

And like a tidal wave, more will stand in their light, until the entire world is flooded with light.

∞

You think you are afraid of your shadow, but what you are most afraid of is your light. Fear of embodying your light can sound like:

~ 'Who am I to think that I can…'
~ 'If I start shining, I will trigger others or leave them behind.'
~ 'What if they think I'm "too much" or full of myself?'
~ 'It's possible for others, but not for me.'
~ 'It's too good to be true. It's not realistic.'
~ 'I'm not ready to handle the visibility, responsibility, or judgment that comes from shining my light.'
~ 'I'll make others uncomfortable if I speak my truth.'
~ 'The thought of actually being free, happy, and in my power is terrifying.'

- 'I won't live up to their (and my) expectations.'
- 'It's safer to not try.'

You know your light is calling you when you teeter-totter between excitement about what's possible and paralyzing doubt. Your doubt is actually an indication that you are on the right track. It is literally the gatekeeper standing at the doorway to your light.

Anchoring the Light Activation: Feeling Safe to Shine Your Light

This is a simple practice to adjust your nervous system to begin to feel safe to shine your light.

- Close your eyes and picture the light in your heart spreading throughout your whole body, illuminating it.

- Take a deep breath and send this light to all your loved ones. Envision it expanding with every breath you take, spreading across your town, your country, and then the entire world, enveloping the whole world with your love.

- Let it expand even more, and send it out into the entire universe, the multiverse that you are.

- See yourself as the entire quantum field, shimmering in light. Breathe deeply, and say out loud:

> *It is safe to shine my light.*
> *I am good enough, just as I am.*
> *It is safe to be seen.*
> *It feels good to be me.*
> *I am the light.*

You can add any other declarations that feel expansive to you. Your vision and intentions are powerful – you create simply by imagining it and feeling the truth of this frequency in your heart.

Standing in Your Power

Your light isn't just your softness. It is your power. It is the full strength of who you are. Standing in your power is about how you show up and walk through the world as the light.

Up to now, it has been easier for you to be kind and loving. This has allowed you to feel safe and be liked. But it has been hard to be seen in your power. And the love that you hold in your heart isn't just gentle. It is fierce, powerful, unafraid to be seen. You have always had a gentle heart, and you will always have your softness. But now you are ready to know the power of your heart.

It is time to fully claim and stand in your power. This flame in you is ready to burn all the illusions of who you are not, all the ways you give your power away, and everything that is not in alignment with your soul. And this means holding that flame high and letting yourself stand out, speak your truth, and shine your light so brightly that it fills the entire world.

When you embody your light, you will no longer hold back, make yourself small, or worry about what others think. You will speak without fear, with love and full clarity. You will know that you – Source – are always guiding yourself.

When you stand in your true power, you will always be connected to your heart. You will always be loving and compassionate, so you will never lose that connection. But you will also be unafraid to let yourself take up space. And this might ruffle some feathers. You may speak truths that others are not ready for yet or shine in a way that makes them uncomfortable. But it is not your responsibility to make others feel comfortable.

> *Let go of the need to blend in,*
> *be liked, or fit others' expectations*
> *of who you should be.*

You are here to crack hearts wide open, and sometimes this can be done with your softness, but often your light is the flame that lets others feel the heat. And even though they may be triggered, it plants a seed. That might just be the seed that helps them bloom into recognizing the light within themselves – in their own time, when it's right for their path.

It's not your job to try to awaken or activate others; this just happens when you are all that you are. Your inner power isn't power over anyone else, it's the highest love and truth of who you are. Claim your power and be free in it. Feel the strength of it coursing through you.

Taking Back Your Power

Look at all the ways you give your power away. You give your power away whenever you agree to any belief or way of being that isn't aligned with the truth of your soul. You may give your power away to friends and family, letting their opinions and expectations push you down… or to disempowering beliefs that do not serve you, feeding the energy of lack and fear... or to money, outer authorities, or systems, thinking they control you.

You give your power away to everything that makes you feel less than the Source that you are. But none of these things actually have power over you; feeling powerless is an experience you create by agreeing to give your power away.

Journal Prompts: Taking Back Your Power

Ask yourself:

+ Where do I still play small?
+ What people, situations, habits, or patterns are draining me? What are they showing me?
+ In what ways do I hide or dim my light?
+ Where am I still choosing what's safe, instead of listening to my heart?
+ What am I still accepting in my life that I don't want to accept?
+ Where am I still feeding the ego battles or narratives of lack, blame, and victimhood in my life?

You begin taking your power back when you catch yourself in disempowering moments and ask yourself:

~ 'How does this make me feel and how do I want to feel?'
~ 'Does this align with my soul?'

- 'What do I need to do to honor the truth of my soul? What changes do I need to make?'
- 'What am I ready to let go?'

This is how you collapse old realities and make room for the new – by letting go of the beliefs, ways of being, and situations that are weighing you down.

Humans struggle with making changes. But when you say 'No more,' you collapse a reality that is no longer aligned with you. It may have served you well up until now, but you're ready to let go of it. And this allows you to open up to a flood of brand-new realities.

If you waver and say you want one thing while your actions display the opposite, your reality will also be wishy-washy. You will continue to feel stuck in the things you want to be free of because you keep choosing them through your actions.

When your thoughts and actions align with the truth of your soul, that's when new realities can be magnetized to you. Most of these changes will be in you. Once you decide what you will no longer put up with, your frequency creates an energetic boundary. For example, you may choose to no longer allow blame, shame, self-judgment, disrespect, or victimhood in your reality. It's up to you to decide what energies you will no longer play in.

When you know your worth, you will no longer put up with situations or ways of being that aren't in alignment with who you are. You won't even have to choose to let them go; they will simply dissolve from your experience, because you won't accept this frequency in your reality anymore.

This will ripple out into the changes you will feel called to make in your life… whether they involve lovingly letting go of people who no longer align with you, speaking up about a need, or distancing yourself from certain situations.

In some situations, you might need to speak up directly, with love, or energetically by simply deciding you're not going to feed that energy anymore. For example, when a friend tries to gossip with you, you can choose not to feed it. Then the conversation either won't go anywhere or will uplevel to a more empowering one. Simply by standing in the full light of who you are and holding yourself and others to a higher frequency, you will collapse the old reality.

These reflections might even shine a spotlight on a bigger change you need to make in life. Perhaps there's something big you've been wanting to do, but you've been holding back out of fear. As terrifying as it may feel, your soul is calling you to lean deeper into trust and take the leap.

> *Any leap in the direction of your soul will be rewarded,*
> *because it is your declaration to your universe:*
> *'I am ready. And I am doing it.'*

Living Your Truth

On this journey, you must let go of wanting to be liked and fit in. No more sacrificing who you are to fit the situation. No more holding back. No more hiding your zest for life, your vision of what is possible, and your inner knowing. All of it is a gift.

Look at all the ways in your life you slightly adjust what you say to be more relatable to others. Notice when your throat tightens out of fear of speaking up or saying what you really mean.

Anchoring the Light Activation: Speaking Your Truth

It is time to activate your throat so you can unleash your voice and speak your truth.

- The first step is to speak your truth to yourself. Be brutally honest. Where aren't you listening to yourself? What aren't you admitting to yourself?

- Then, practice speaking more freely to friends who are on the same wavelength as you and don't judge you.

- Expand this practice into your wider circles, witnessing any fears that come up.

Speaking your truth is a concept that has been misunderstood by many. It's not about pushing your opinions down other people's throats, defending yourself, or trying to change or convince others from an energy of force. It's about being aligned with your soul and honoring your frequency as well as others'.

When you're aligned in this way, you'll know what to say and what not to say. Sometimes, you'll know the best thing is not to say anything at all – not to feed the energy of ego, mind games, and debates that just go round in circles. You'll know where your energy wants to go and the highest-frequency choice you can make, which may be either to say something from the heart or gently remove yourself from a situation that feels heavy. You'll let others be themselves, without needing to change them. And at the same time, you'll be fully yourself – without sacrificing any of your light.

When you're holding space for a friend or family member who is struggling, speaking your truth is not about being blindly positive without empathy. When you come from the heart, you'll naturally be compassionate, listen, and hold space for their human self. At the same time, you'll see the light in them and won't play in disempowerment, victimhood, or blame anymore. You won't feed these stories.

You aren't here to dull your frequency to meet others where they're at. You're here to hold the light at your true frequency, so that others can choose to rise, too. Sometimes, your light helps others come back to their hearts, let go of their limitations, and see themselves as the light that they are. You may do this through words, but mostly it happens simply through your presence. Your frequency activates others, even if they don't feel it consciously. Sometimes, they aren't ready. And that is okay.

When speaking to certain friends, you might notice you focus more on sharing your human struggles and doubts, even though your heart knows everything's working out. Your heart knows you aren't a victim of your fears, but maybe you play the victim so that others can feel comfortable in their victimhood. And when you want to speak about all the goodness in your life, you hold back. This is another way you dim your light.

Maybe you hold yourself back in your creations and what you share with the world. You want to shine just enough to still be accepted. You let yourself dance within the confines of what people expect of you. But this must be getting boring for you now, because your being wants to play in what is new. Give yourself the freedom to be who you came here to be in your unique way.

The quirkiest parts of you that don't make sense to others are your greatest strengths… your true essence… and your soul's light shining through. Be the light of Source that you are. No one else can give you permission to be this. Only you can give it to yourself.

Let yourself expand, and then get bigger. Let yourself dream big. Hold the highest vision for yourself and the world. Notice when you don't let yourself envision the highest possibility out of fear that it might not work out. You may tell yourself it's better to be realistic and not get your hopes up, but tune back in to your heart and let yourself receive the full frequency of what is possible, knowing that the highest possible realities are coming in. It doesn't matter how your vision happens, or what the outcome looks like. This is about having faith that it is possible. It is done.

> *Instead of waiting for something to happen, step forth and claim it.*

Instead of yearning for something that is not here, melt into this moment. 'I am here. I am here. I am here. And it is done.' Go further, and let yourself dream even bigger. Go beyond your wildest dreams. No more being realistic. If you feel your dreams are a bit delusional, you're on the right track. Keep dreaming bigger than that. You're only scratching the surface of what is possible.

As your frequency shifts, your entire reality shifts. As you break all limitations, you become limitless. As you embody more of your light, you become a magnet, attracting everything. You are what you've been waiting for.

Channeling Your Soul

Another way to get to know and trust your inner power is to bask in the frequency of your higher self and Source, through meditation and channeling.

In the world, there are many examples of people who channel messages from their guides, higher self, angels, or other inter-dimensional beings, who are aspects of themselves. It is called 'channeling' because it's a way of becoming a conduit for higher-frequency wisdom and messages.

But as you embody more of your light, you no longer have the experience of receiving guidance from outside of yourself. It was never really coming from there; you just perceived it that way because you viewed your higher self as outside of yourself. Now, you're ready to open up to a new way of channeling, which is simply channeling yourself as Source, channeling your soul.

Anchoring the Light Activation: Channeling Your Soul

How do you channel yourself?

Speaking out loud

You can play with this practice until it feels natural to you to simply tune in and connect at any moment.

- At first, it helps to find a quiet place with no distractions. Lie down, close your eyes, and take a few deep breaths. Tune in to the stillness and love in your heart.

- Breathing deeply, relax your body, and set the intention to connect with yourself as Source.

- Imagine the light in your heart blooming with every breath, expanding outward. This is the light of Source, within you. (You can also listen to a guided meditation for this part if it helps you drop in more.)

- When you feel calm and relaxed (you will notice your mind becoming more quiet), you can ask yourself – as Source – a question. It helps to speak out loud, as if you are having a conversation with yourself.

Speak slowly in a relaxed way, as if you're guiding yourself in a meditation. Start with a simple question, one that you don't care about as much, because this will help you get into the flow. For instance, 'What am I ready to let go of now?' Or 'Why have I been feeling off lately?' Ask whatever is relevant to you.

- Keep breathing deeply, and trust the first feeling or thought that arises, without second-guessing it. Begin to speak out loud, as Source, answering your own question.

You might find it feels natural to answer your question talking about yourself in the second person, i.e. 'You are ready to let go of…' It is a conversation between you as a human and you as Source. In the beginning, it might just be a short sentence or word or two that comes through. It is completely normal to feel stuck or notice your mind trying to think of the answer. Keep breathing deeply and speaking out loud, and your channeling will get stronger as you get into the flow.

If you feel completely stuck, you can ask yourself as Source, 'Why am I feeling stuck?' Shining a light on what you're resisting or what's coming up for you in the moment often helps you move past any blocks. Just start talking, even if it feels like your mind is making it up. Let go of second-guessing yourself, and as you get more comfortable, you'll notice the words start to flow more easily. The more you trust it, the more it will bloom.

- And when you're ready, you can ask a bigger question.

It may help to record these sessions using a voice recorder app on your phone, so that you can listen to them later and not worry about using your analytical mind to remember everything you're saying.

It also greatly helps to do this where no one else can overhear or disturb you, so that you don't feel self-conscious.

Even with simple questions, when you're in this relaxed channeling state, you'll notice the answers that come through are clear and often offer a higher, more balanced, perspective. They will come with comfort, encouragement, and love.

This is the voice of your soul, and you will recognize it.

Automatic writing

You can do this practice through automatic writing, too. This is especially useful if you find journaling easier than speaking out loud.

- Prepare a pen and paper or page on your laptop, and drop into a meditative state.
- Set the intention to connect with yourself as Source.
- At the top of the page, write down your first question.
- Then, as much as you can without thinking, start writing the first thought or feeling that comes through in response to your question. Keep writing, without editing or judging what's coming through.

- When it feels complete, you can write down another question, and keep going.

This is a beautiful way to tune in to the highest perspectives and frequency available around any question or situation in your life. As you do this, you will gain more confidence in your soul connection and trust that you have the ability to guide yourself through anything.

Before long, this practice will become easier for you and you won't need to spend a long time in meditation to quieten your mind and drop into this space. Sometimes you'll just close your eyes and take three deep breaths, and away you'll go. You can play with this and find what suits you best.

Eventually, you'll realize you don't even need to close your eyes to channel yourself out loud. This connection is with you at all times. Of course, it helps to close your eyes to get rid of the distractions, or to sit in nature. But the connection already exists.

Less than five years ago, I didn't know what it would be like to receive clear guidance from my soul or trust in that connection. I was awed by people who could channel messages from their soul, higher self, or 'spirit guides' and receive the answer to any question they had. I thought they had a special gift that I did not.

It took me a while to realize that I could do the same… that I was already channeling through my writing, without realizing it… and that everyone has this ability. It's just that our own doubt and mental filtering get in the way of trusting it. For me, it wasn't an ability that showed up out of the blue one day, it was something I connected with over time.

Shortly after I moved to Perth, Western Australia to be with Joel, I made my first two friends in Australia. Every month or so, we would gather at someone's house, have dinner, and then do an impromptu cacao ceremony as part of our girls' night.

The ceremonies evolved over time, but we naturally stepped into different roles. One friend would open the ceremony with her big shamanic drum. Another (usually me) would guide the dreaming journey, a meditation with various components: declaring our intentions for the month ahead, connecting with our higher self, letting go of our fears, visualizing our dreams, and so on. Another friend would close the ceremony with powerful kundalini mantras and energy-clearing breathwork.

It was such a fun way to support each other and share our hopes and dreams, fears, and most vulnerable thoughts. These friendships made me feel at home in a land far away from home. In this relaxed and safe space, I would feel my heart soaring open, warmth spreading through my chest. These ceremonies took us into a higher frequency, and it was common for us to receive insights, clarity, and ideas throughout. I began to recognize these as messages from the soul.

Over time, I played around with different ways of guiding the ceremonies and dropping us into our hearts. Of course, I was nervous at first and felt like I was totally winging it. But in this safe space, I could practice trusting whatever wanted to come through, without planning what to say beforehand.

We started inviting more friends to join, and sometimes there were six to eight people there. I began to be asked to guide ceremonies for various friends' rites of passage or other events: birthdays, a wedding, a retreat, and a going-away party. I was extremely nervous, but I gained confidence with each one. These were no longer simple guided meditative journeys. They became spaces for deep energetic clearing, letting go of lifetimes of fears and programming, receiving messages from our souls, anchoring our light, and more.

One day, I offered my first online guided ceremony on Zoom, and eight people showed up. I was nervous about doing it without the in-person element, but it went smoothly, and the energy felt equally potent.

After a few months, I started consistently offering live online ceremonies, followed by an open Q&A. They grew in size from 70 people to 200, to my biggest one, 800 people tuning in from all over the world. Through these ceremonies, I taught people how to channel their higher self, trust in their own guidance, and embody their light.

In the beginning, because of nerves, I would reflect on the theme beforehand and write down a rough ceremony outline on a page in my notebook. Over time, I stopped needing this notebook and started guiding ceremonies on the fly, reading into the energy of the group and trusting the inspiration that came through as I went. At the best times, I felt like I wasn't leading the ceremony, I was receiving it. I realized I was channeling the ceremonies, even the answers to the Q&A questions.

This is how I started trusting the voice of my soul: by getting to know the energy of my higher self and speaking as her. It helped strengthen my trust in my writing, allowing me to give validity to whatever words came through, without second-guessing them.

These ceremonies also helped me trust my unique essence. I didn't try to lead them like anyone else. I trusted my heart to shine through and my frequency to hold the space – and this was the energy that was transmitted and shared with everyone, more than the words I said.

What struck me most was the fact that this connection with my soul's guidance felt no different from the higher perspectives that would often come through in my journal entries, even from childhood, or in deep conversations with friends. I realized that I had always been connected and guided, as we all are. It was time to trust it.

Those of you who have been tuning in and receiving messages for a while may notice your connection with spirit and guidance is changing. Many people refer to the spontaneous messages they receive from spirit as 'downloads.' And in the beginning of your journey, you may have felt these downloads were much more profound. When they came in, you could feel the expansiveness of the energy behind the message. This was because the frequency of the download was so much higher than the frequency you held in your body. And because of this contrast, it felt uplifting to receive the message.

Now, your frequency is much higher than before. And so, as you embody the light of your higher self more and more, the way you connect to your guidance changes. You might not feel like you're having groundbreaking 'Aha!' moments anymore. You might feel like your guidance has gone quiet. You might feel like you're more disconnected, even though you are more connected than ever before. This is only because the way you are receiving guidance is completely changing. Instead of Earth-shattering downloads, you're finding you already know what you need to know. The answers come to the surface more subtly, but with clarity, as if they're your own thoughts. And they are – because you are much more embodied and grounded in your knowing. Your channeling may feel just like the voice in your head. But you will know it's not your programmed mind speaking; there is a clearer, higher quality to the energy coming through.

Let go of expecting the way you connect to energy or spirit to feel the same as it did before, even six months or one year ago. You don't need guiding messages anymore when you just know what you need to know. Of course, you can still tune in and set the intention to receive guidance from yourself, from your universe, from the Source that you are, whenever you want. But you are always connected to your inner truth – and the light of your soul, your highest wisdom, always shines through when you're in your heart.

When you're in a flowing conversation, giving encouragement and advice to a friend, you are channeling yourself. When you're experiencing insights while journaling, you're channeling yourself. When you're painting or singing from the heart, you're channeling yourself, translating energy into form.

Claim this now: you are your highest self. You are embodied. You have anchored the light so you can know yourself as the light of God in physical form. And so, you are no longer channeling; you are simply being in your connection at all times. This is just who you are now.

You might feel as human as before. You might feel like you're still stuck in your struggles, worries, and doubts. But at the same time, you know something has shifted. If you just tune in to your heart, you can find more calm there. Even if the worries and fears come up, you can witness them now. And instead of letting them drag you down, more often than not, you can see them for what they are. Despite these thoughts, your heart is calm. Your energy field is pristine. You can find that peace within.

True connection is knowing who you are... walking in your truth, with deep trust in yourself, solidly anchored in who you are. Notice how much you have changed as you have embodied who you are. You don't put up with anything that doesn't align with your soul anymore. You honor your energy and what you need. You listen to yourself now.

Your connection to your spirit and all that you are is stronger than it has ever been, because you have never been more solid in who you are, more trusting in life and yourself, more unswayed by others' opinions.

You know you have shifted massively when you no longer see your challenges, triggers, or 'negative' emotions as bad, but as lessons, gifts, and opportunities to see what you couldn't see before in yourself and move the density out. You not only see the light in the light; you also see the light in the shadow. There is no positive or negative; you see it all as divinely perfect.

And though all of this might feel less mystical and more normal at times, it's still absolutely beautiful, because this is the place you've been yearning to be in – knowing who you are, being the light that you are, walking through the world as your light. It isn't something you need to reach for anymore. It is just who you are.

Unbecoming

Becoming *more* can also feel like unbecoming. Letting go. Unraveling. Throughout your journey, you've been measuring your spiritual and personal growth by how much you're shifting, healing, learning, and growing. But in this season, your growth may look and feel different. It may not be about becoming more, improving yourself, or solidifying the foundation of who you are… but about unbecoming.

> *Embrace the unraveling. Tell yourself,*
> *'I let go. To become, I must first unbecome.'*

If you built the old you with hard work and effort, the emergence of the new you might feel like nothing much is happening at all. You are not adding more masks and identities to cling to – instead, you're stripping them away. You're not putting more beliefs and noise into your head, you are letting it all go. You're not necessarily *trying* to become new, it is simply *happening*. You are getting to know the strength in the softness of the new you.

Every illusion must crumble when you awaken to who you are, and it's okay to grieve your old self, even the dreams of your old self. It's okay to not yet trust your new self, or even know where you are heading. It's okay if you feel lost, when you thought you had found your footing. You are never truly lost when your home is in your heart.

In this unraveling, there will come a point when you don't care what you believe anymore… because instead of fortifying your beliefs, you're experiencing what it's like to have fewer beliefs. And with this comes less rigidity, less attachment to how things have to be.

Instead of gaining progress and momentum, clarity and breakthroughs, you're doing less. Simplifying. Trying less hard. Slowing down. Letting go. Being okay with not making outward progress. Getting comfortable with the discomfort. Letting go of attachments and control. Not fearing as much, which can feel like not caring as much. Letting go of physicality, as you prioritize your inner world.

When you let go of people-pleasing, trying to be good enough, comparing yourself to others, feeling behind, hustling to get ahead… when you stop trying to control everything and be perfect… what is left?

You are left with yourself – the pure essence of yourself. Then you start loving yourself and accepting yourself as you are, and with this comes a deep relief.

> *There is nothing to do but be yourself.*
> *There is a simplicity and beauty there,*
> *if you let yourself melt into it.*

You are becoming less attached to how you define yourself and your role in the world. Your identity is unraveling… even the identities you've worked so hard to build.

You are letting go of caring so much about the perceptions of others, as well as your self-perceptions, even labels you may resonate with, like 'spiritual,' 'lightworker,' 'truth-seeker,' 'mystic.' Maybe you once needed to be these things to find a place for yourself in the world. But over time, you'll find you're happy if the labels morph and merge, and even melt away. You are constantly expanding, and you cannot be defined by any label. You're just happy to be yourself.

Even the idea of shining your light may shift in its pull. Instead of needing to shine your light to be seen, to make a difference in the world, you begin resting in the knowing that you already shine your light, just by being yourself. It is a natural by-product of who you are.

You are also being called to dissolve the savior complex, thinking you need to save others, fix the systems, or change the world. Though it's coming from your heart, it carries an undercurrent of seeing lack and limitation in the world, feeling like you need to save others or else they are doomed… But now you are coming into the knowing that every soul is whole, guided, and on their path. The world is changing in perfect orchestration.

Just by being yourself, you'll naturally keep shining your light, sharing your gifts, and helping those around you – but this will simply be because it is your joy, it is an expression of who you are.

When you're happy with who you are, when you see and love yourself fully, you'll no longer feel the need to prove yourself and be seen. You'll know that you are whole, you are enough, you are magnificent… and though you'll appreciate it when others acknowledge you, you won't need them to see you.

Most people are focused on becoming more, so this world doesn't value the tremendous courage of unbecoming. The paradox is, when you truly let go of trying to become, you finally become all that you are.

Your Light Is Needed

This journey will push you to get more comfortable with your light. You may begin to feel like you're okay with a certain level of being seen and living your truth… but there are more layers of doubt to clear. Keep going, keep expanding into all that you are, and those layers of density will be alchemized into full trust in yourself, until one day you will be jumping to shine the full light of who you are.

You will realize that claiming your light isn't actually outside your comfort zone, it's the truth of who you are. And it's the safest, most freeing place to be.

So, let yourself shine,
beautiful soul.

Even during this time of great chaos and suffering on Earth, *especially* during this time, your light is needed more than ever before. You cannot lift the suffering into a higher dimension by sitting in the same frequency. You are here to bring the highest frequencies of love, hope, and possibility to Earth, and this is what allows your reality to expand into new ideas, solutions, and ways of being that match the highest frequencies you are anchoring now. This is how you stream the light of Source onto Earth.

You've always been a vessel for Source. But because you didn't remember this, in many ways you closed your connection, so the light of Source could not fully stream through your body and out into the world.

Now, you're embodying who you truly are. This allows the connection to open fully and the energy of all that you are to flow through you… allowing light to stream through you and out into the reality you are creating… shining the light of God on Earth.

And so, be the light that you know yourself to be. Be the living embodiment of Source. Bring the light of all that you are into your body, into this moment, onto the Earth. Be yourself, and walk in the knowing that you are the light.

Everything you embody and activate within you ripples out into your reality, freely and abundantly. And as you walk through life and hold the knowing that you are Source, you will stream the light of Source into the world – no matter what you are doing, and even when you are doing nothing at all.

CHAPTER 11

Creating as the Quantum Field

Simply by existing, you create. In every moment, you are creating the reality that is reflected back to you. Today, most people view creating through the vehicle of their work, purpose, or hobbies – but it is so much bigger than that. In this chapter, we will explore how the way you create your reality is completely changing… and how this will change the way you view work, purpose, and all of your creations as you step into the New Earth.

For your entire history, work has been about surviving – making enough to get by and providing for yourself and your family. At the core, it has been about money – the money that you need to survive and live as you'd like to on this planet.

Of course, many receive other benefits from their work, like fulfillment, growth, purpose, connections with others, structure, and more. The vehicle of work allows you to expand as a soul and experience more facets of who you are. At the same time, even those who are doing work that they love are only scratching the surface of what is truly possible for them when they let go of the old programming and beliefs around work and purpose.

Much of work, including work that feels fulfilling, is still rooted in the old paradigm of needing money to survive, fueled by the energies of lack and scarcity. It is still predominantly based on the linear way of thinking, where you must trade your time and energy for money.

There are many limitations with this, because despite how hard you work and how much you may earn, it can still feel like there's not enough. There's always further to go, more to do, more to earn. And this carries an underlying energy of stress, competition, and struggle.

You are dismantling the entire paradigm of what it means to be alive on this Earth, dissolving the entire belief system around having to earn a living, the ability to exist.

It was never supposed to be about the struggle to survive, eat, or have a roof over your head on a planet that is actually abundant in ways beyond anything you have been told. Those controlling the systems of the world, including government, banking, and the media, have kept humanity locked in the denser energies of lack and scarcity – trapping you in cycles of debt and excessive taxation, pushing the fear that there's not enough for all to survive, let alone thrive, on Earth.

In truth, this planet has more than enough for everyone, especially when resources are properly distributed and new technologies released that can solve your planet's most pressing problems. When all beings are connected to their soul and living from their heart, you will create a world overflowing with generosity. You will come up with new ways to grow food and share resources. All the systems that have kept humanity in an endless cycle of scarcity and lack will be replaced by supportive systems.

The New Earth you are creating is one where all beings can live freely and thrive, knowing exactly who they are, connected to their spirit. The frequency of the Earth is shifting, along with yours, because, like everything, the Earth is a consciousness that interacts with you. The way you interact with the Earth will change, and you will live in harmony with the land.

Ultimately, you will see that all of these changes start with you. When you tap into the quantum field, you can magnetize to you anything you wish to experience or need. You are stepping into a brand-new reality where you will experience abundance, limitlessness, and possibility beyond any human concept that you have known.

Magnetism

How is this possible? The way you experience creating your reality has been distorted because of old ideas around manifestation, and the interference of the limiting belief systems that keep you in doubt.

For the most part, manifestation has been seen and taught as a practice for attracting what you desire. And conventionally, this has been mostly focused on attracting material things, like money, or your heart's desires, like a romantic partner.

And while many manifestation practices allow you to get in the energy and feeling of what it is you wish to experience, they still hold the assumption that you are separate from what you wish to experience… that what you want to call in is not yet here, and so it is outside of you. You have experienced manifestation as challenging, especially around the things you desire most, as they seem to take a long time to come in, or not come in at all.

This makes it feel like you have to do all this hard work around manifestation practices, visioning, and working on your mindset to pull it in. And while many of the practices and perspectives around manifestation do work, and have worked for millions of people, it is time to upgrade the frequency you hold around the idea.

Instead of manifestation, begin to look at it as magnetism. Instead of trying to attract something from outside, turn your gaze inward. Magnetism is about becoming a magnet, becoming the entire quantum field, instantaneously drawing to you everything you need in every moment, from your own energetic field.

> *You are everything, so everything you wish to experience already exists within you.*

You hold the keys to unlock that frequency, timeline, and reality. Abundance exists within you, because you *are* abundance. Love exists within you, because you are love.

Creation isn't about pulling your desires in from outside. It's about tuning yourself to that frequency within. When you do this, you will see your outer world shift to reflect the frequency you have found within.

Unlike manifestation, magnetism doesn't require practices or tools. Instead of manifesting through your mind, you magnetize through your embodied frequency – through knowing, trusting, and being all that you are. It happens naturally through you, as you embody the frequency of what you desire and choose to experience in life, knowing it is already done. And because it is done, you don't have to worry about how or when it will happen. You can just let go and enjoy the now.

When you have a specific dream or desire you want to magnetize, you don't need to visualize the details or repeat them in your head. Let go of trying to control it from your mind, because that is rooted in lack. Instead, trust that your soul already knows the energy and feeling of what you want. Trust that it is already unfolding, better than you can plan.

The key is to surrender, and step into total faith in the flow of your universe. Tell yourself, 'If it happens the way I want, great. If it doesn't, something better is unfolding.' Let go of control.

This book has walked you through the journey – sitting with your shadows, clearing the density and fears, anchoring the light, and stepping into total faith in the divine – so that you can become a magnetic being. You are one already, and your ability to magnetize will heighten until it becomes your daily experience of creating in life.

The greatest shift available is this: Instead of always waiting for a future moment to come, feel complete and whole in the present moment. You have everything you need in this moment. It is perfect. And from that space, every moment that follows will also be whole and complete.

When you know that you are everything, you are never in lack. When you know nothing is missing, your outer reality will reflect this. Remember, your outer reality is a projection of you. When you realize this, you will know that there is nothing you cannot experience. It is up to you to hold that knowing within in order to see it reflected back to you. Everything you do from that place will be of a different frequency from anything you experienced when you were in lack and separation.

You will feel free to do whatever you want. Be however you want. And you will feel so excited to experience and express all that you are, in the way that feels most joyful to you in every moment.

You will be inspired to create because it's fun and fulfilling. You will be moved to share because you love your community and the world, and you want to contribute. Many will feel thrilled to bring their visions to life, build new structures, join together behind causes and projects, and serve in ways that light them up. It will all be for your life, your community, and the world that you are building.

But it will feel like an effortless extension of yourself, just being yourself, showing up in every moment. It will come from the free-flowing inspiration of the soul and the deliciousness of experiencing all that you are, and different aspects of yourself, as you continue to expand.

The reason the way you are experiencing manifesting is changing is because you are stepping into the full truth of who you are and claiming it. You will experience untapped creativity flowing through you, because this is who you are.

You create. You are a creator. You've always been creating from your belief systems, just not as consciously. There's no way you could experience this life without that, because all of it is a creation of your consciousness.

The paradox is, only when you stop trying to control your reality will you see that you actually create your reality. And you don't need to try to control it anymore. Instead, let go and trust the frequency that you are to bring in everything you need. The momentum shifts, from forcefully creating to harnessing your inner power.

Creating on the New Earth

What you do on the New Earth won't feel like work in the way you have known it. It will feel like being fully yourself – and everything you create from that space will be an extension of yourself... an exploration of an expression or idea of yourself that excites you. What you create will be a natural expression of yourself – loving life, being love, sharing your essence in whatever way you like.

People get stuck with this question: 'How do I translate what I love into what I do?' But this is limiting, because it carries the wrong assumptions:

- Thinking what you love has to be defined within a role, single purpose, or identity.
- Thinking the goal is to figure out what you will *do*, when it is about discovering who you *are* and how you want to *feel*.
- Thinking you have to know the answer first in order to begin, when in truth, you just start by following the breadcrumbs of your excitement, and the path will show itself as you go.
- Thinking what you do will look a certain way, when it will actually expand as you expand.

On the New Earth, what you do and create is:

- led by the heart, and not the mind
- coming from a place of excitement, not fear
- not led by what the audience or customers want, but by what your heart wants to experience
- not primarily led by the question: 'How do I make money?'

- not twisted or stunted to fit within the system
- guided by synchronicity, inspiration, and joy
- not bound by rules
- supportive of your highest good and that of humanity

Paradoxically, when you don't make it about the money, you open up to inspiration and a new way of being that will allow you not only to get by, but to thrive.

> *When you follow your heart and keep stepping in alignment with your soul, you will experience abundance beyond anything you have known.*

But the catalyst will be an energy of excitement and possibility, not lack or fear. And when you serve your own soul first, you will find your greatest capacity to serve the world.

You might be questioning what truly excites you, and find that nothing tangible feels right. But your highest contribution to the world isn't found in what you create physically, it's in what you do energetically – simply by being yourself. This can feel frustrating, because you have an innate desire to create, offer your gifts, and see your impact. But even your best ideas may feel heavy, not enough, not quite 'it.'

When this happens, your most exciting ideas are still being filtered – translated – to fit something practical for the physical world that you know today. But your highest ideas come from your soul – dimensions beyond this physical reality – and they are more of a *feeling* than a tangible blueprint. When your mind tries to create the blueprint, it applies the limitations and expectations of your current reality. And so, the expansive energy – the pure joy – of what you truly want to experience becomes constricted. If you get bogged down in the details and plans, you will lose the pure energy behind the vision.

Journal Prompts: Your Creations

Your most radiant creations will come from these types of questions:

- How do I want to experience and express all that I am?
- What do I want to activate and explore within myself?
- How do I want to share my heart with the world?
- Is there a fun and easeful way to do it?
- If I could do anything, what would I want to do?
- How do I want to feel in my life?

When you start here, you allow yourself to come from the purest place, and all the next steps and logistical questions will be answered without needing to overthink them. Let your heart lead, and all the parts needed to fulfill the vision of all that you are and what you are creating will come in. It won't feel like you're pulling them in by force. It will feel like you are simply answering the call of what you're inspired to do, in every moment.

Your 'work' won't be confined by the limitations of one suite of products or services. It won't even be a replica of something you have already created in the past. It will be an ever-evolving reflection of your expanding excitement, curiosities, and gifts.

As you expand upon your own idea of who you are, your creations will naturally expand. You will gravitate toward exploring the frontiers of your imagination, consciousness, and energy. You will create because you want to discover who you are – in the process and on the other side.

You won't be creating to prove something or be perceived a certain way, but because of how it makes you feel… how it makes your heart sing. Your work will be a seamless part of living the life of your dreams… In fact, it will no longer be 'work.' That word will fade from your consciousness. What you create will simply allow you to thrive and grow beyond anything you have ever known.

You will see it as your joy. The devotion of your heart. An offering to the world that you love. 'This is what I'd be doing if I could do anything… this is who I'd be. This is who I am.' The inner work you have been doing to step into who you truly are is the greatest foundation and fuel for your wildest dreams.

The Gift of Your Frequency

Ultimately, your purpose is not about what you do or create… but about being fully yourself. It is about your frequency – the frequency that you embody, the energy that emanates from you when you know all the light that you are. This is what ripples out and has the highest impact on you and the reality around you, regardless of what you're doing or not doing.

Your frequency is your highest gift to yourself and the world. Your frequency is everything, because you are energy. That is all there is.

You are moving from seeing the world through the lens of physicality to seeing the world through the lens of energy. This will open up to a new way of interacting with your reality through frequency. You will see that your frequency is what shifts and creates your reality. As time bends and dissolves, you will see how you can instantaneously create and shift realities.

This ability to shift between realities is exponentially more powerful than the culmination of many physical actions taken over time. If you try to change your outer reality just through physical effort and action, you will be creating in the old way through struggle, force, and effort. This way takes a lot of time, and you will only be able to create within the confines of the frequency that the action you take comes from. When you realize everything starts with energy and you allow your embodiment of the frequency of all that you are, and all that is possible, to be at the forefront, you will draw to you everything you need. You will be able to create anything that you can imagine, and it will be as if it is coming to you and moving through you with total ease.

The frequency is what does the 'doing.' The frequency is what does the hard work for you while you just let yourself *be*. This frequency is what rearranges timelines and brings your highest path to you. It creates trust in the life you are creating and excitement about who you are and who you are becoming, magnetizing your wildest dreams to you.

This is the new way – creating from the energy of who you truly are, not from the illusions of all that you are not. You don't need to dip into the noise of struggle and doubt, and the mental chatter of *Should I do this or that? Am I doing enough?* or *What are 10 other things I should do?* All of this feels dense and heavy to you for a reason: because it is no longer the dimension you are wanting to exist in.

A LETTER FROM YOUR SOUL

Dear sweet soul,

You're worried about money, and it's one of those things that has always had a tight grip on you. Throughout your life, whether you've had just enough or more than enough, you've been worried about the future... wondering, 'What if something happens, what if it runs out, what if I can't build a better life?'

Somehow, you've always been supported, but this fear has kept you in your head – the familiar tightness in your chest, urging you to worry, worry, worry. You wonder if you'll ever be free of this. You would give anything to be free of this.

If you could glimpse the life that's coming for you, even for a split second, you'd drop all your worries at once. You'd be astonished to see how quickly your life is already changing, how all your dreams are coming in faster than you can keep up with them, how utterly supported you are... and how you don't even need to think about money, because you will discover your inherent worth – which is your frequency. Your essence. The unique wisdom, power, and gifts of your soul.

Your frequency is your wealth, because it brings you everything you need. It is the gift that keeps on giving, because the energy of being who you truly are in this world is priceless. It is your greatest value; everything you do, say, and create from this space is of the highest value.

Others will flock to you, just to be around your energy. People, resources, and support will flood in, just to be part of making your visions come to life. You will unlock an infinite well of creativity, wisdom, and love within you that overflows into everything you touch.

Everything you're doing now to embody your light is your greatest investment in yourself. You are standing at the leading edge of humanity's ascension, and you cannot yet see the millions upon millions who are awakening now, all around the world. This is a revolution that will touch every soul on the planet. In time, billions will be awakening, seeking answers, seeking the light.

And there will be no greater offering than your frequency. You, embodying the light, standing in the new, showing the world what is possible for all. This is everything.

With love,
Your soul

Even when you're relaxing, enjoying yourself without a care in the world, your frequency ripples out. It anchors more light and love on Earth. It shifts your planet. It shifts your humanity. And you will know that simply being yourself is your greatest joy and offering.

You'll see beauty in every moment and realize that everything is absolutely perfect. And from this place of peace, you will know that just *being* is everything. There's so much depth here. And who you are in that space is absolutely exquisite. You will feel more alive, more yourself, more lit up, more in love with life and the world than you have ever felt.

And as you walk through the world, others will be able to feel this energy. You will see it reflected back to you. You will know there's absolutely nothing that is out of place. There is nowhere you have to go, nowhere you have to be, but here.

As you melt into this relaxation, this arrival in your life, you will know that allowing yourself to be in this loving presence is more potent than anything you have ever felt. And this is more important than anything you do, because in this space, you'll see how life flows with harmony. You will see how your world comes alive with miracles and magic everywhere you look.

This is a frequency that has barely been tasted, let alone embodied on this planet. This is the greatest frequency to embody at this moment, at this time – for the sake of soaking it in, just being here. And that is true abundance.

The Quickening of Your Creations

As your vibrational frequency rises, your consciousness expands beyond the constraints of this third-dimensional realm. Time begins to dissolve. And so you will notice there is a quickening in your ability to magnetize – a decreasing gap between your desire and its materialization, between your vision and its reality. And this is happening because you are expanding beyond the illusion of time and into all that you are as the quantum field.

It will look like the outer world is responding faster to your energy. You will clearly see the feedback loop between the belief system you hold and the reality you experience. But this will simply be because you are dissolving the illusion of separation between you and the outer world, between your own frequency and the frequency out there. You aren't separate from any experience, creation, or version of yourself that you desire.

Manifestation can also feel like it's speeding up because your sense of worthiness is increasing. You can erase entire steps that you used to think you needed to take to be ready and worthy enough to receive what you desired. Now, if you truly feel ready and worthy, you'll realize nothing is out of reach, and it doesn't have to take so long to receive it.

If the reality you are experiencing isn't what you would prefer, look at any beliefs you may be holding that are creating it. Anytime you notice a fear or belief held in limitation, catch yourself and let yourself expand beyond it. Feel the possibility in your bones. Open your heart to appreciate everything around you. Become the energy of abundance, knowing you are connected to it all.

Expand your idea of what you believe is possible and what you are worthy of.

This is what draws to you the reality that matches the frequency you hold within. This is how it works. It is getting easier to shift because you are expanding exponentially faster than ever before. The fluid nature of reality will become more obvious to you as you play with this idea and begin to see every moment as brand new.

Anchoring the Light Activation: Dreaming Bigger

A powerful practice is taking the pressure, or weight, off your dreams... seeing them more lightly and making them fun. The key is to start playing with the 'what ifs' – not with your fears, as you have done many times before, but with the possibilities.

- ✦ 'It's not out of the realm of possibility that this could happen...'
- ✦ 'What if it all works out even better than I can imagine?'

- 'Of course there's a way that could happen easily...'
- 'Wouldn't it be fun if that happened...?'
- 'What if letting go is the portal to it all?'

Notice what comes in when you begin truly feeling like this. Look at all the ways things have come in for you in the past, especially when you believed they were possible.

Most of the world isn't living like this, because most of the world is fixated on the outer physical reality. People are looking outward, saying, 'Look at all the evidence that things aren't working out!' But they aren't looking inward. And this is what changes everything.

Sometimes, you do want things that aren't aligned with your soul, and your universe has a better path in store for you. Sometimes, you can only understand why things happened a certain way in retrospect. But everything you need for your highest path does come in right when you need it.

And this is abundance – knowing you are provided for and will receive exactly what you need exactly when you need it, not a moment sooner or later. You are anchoring more light every day – and this means you are anchoring more trust.

The way this book, *Anchoring the Light*, came to be may be one of the first memorable tastes of magnetism I've had thus far. Joel and I had come back from visiting my grandma in Japan to the start of winter in Australia. In winter, I usually go more inward, and it's a beautiful time to start a project. I felt this spaciousness and readiness to start something new, but I didn't put any thought into what that could be.

A few hours later, I had a spontaneous thought: *It wouldn't be out of the realm of possibility that an aligned publisher finds my writing on social media and wants to work with me on my second book.*

It was a fleeting thought, accompanied by an air of grounded possibility: *Yeah, that could happen.* It may have been the first time I truly felt it was possible, without attachment to whether, or how, it happened or not. I didn't think too much of it and went about my day.

Literally the next morning, less than 12 hours later, I woke up to a message on Instagram from a woman who wrote: 'I'm reaching out as I work as the Associate Publisher for Hay House, Inc., and wondered if you would have any interest in discussing the possibility of publishing a book with us. I love the messages you share online and think we could help you share that energy with an even wider audience around the world.'

My heart leapt, and I was flooded with wonder at this opportunity, the timing of the message, the clear synchronicity. At the same time, it felt expected – like this was the logical next step. *Oh yeah, I thought about this yesterday.* I recognized Hay House right away, as it was the leading global mind–body–spirit publisher – and I couldn't have dreamed of working with a more aligned publisher. I didn't have to email a long list of publishers and pitch myself. Here was an editor who already loved and appreciated my writing and wanted us to work together.

Over the next three months, I went through the process of having calls with the editor, putting together a 50-page outline and book proposal, and awaiting the green light from the Hay House team. Normally, with something as big as this, I would be nervous about whether it would actually go ahead or not, but because of the divinely synchronistic way the opportunity came to me, I felt quite surrendered and trusting throughout the whole process.

It felt like the book was happening – it was done. Every step felt easeful, as if the inspiration and momentum behind every action I needed to take came in to meet me. Like my first book, this book was channeled from my heart, and much of it came through in channelings that I spoke into a voice recorder app in a meditative state. The app automatically transcribed my words, and I later edited the pages upon pages of channeling.

During the writing of this book, Hay House was acquired by Penguin Random House, which would expand the distribution of the book while still allowing me to work directly with the Hay House branch and my amazing editor.

This experience gave me a taste of what it was like to create with total flow and magnetism. In this state, there is no need to pull anything in by force. Your frequency, readiness, and total knowing in the possibility – without attachment to how it happens – pull everything in for you.

Your soul is in complete faith. And the more you anchor your light and create space for your true self to be embodied, the more you will walk through the world with trust. The highest timeline is the one in which you surrender and trust the flow of life to bring you exactly what you need when you need it. Remember to hold the energy of 'It is already done,' and this will help you to let go. The path of force is no longer working.

> ***Your soul wants you to open up to the full capacity of your being and taste its limitless potential.***

And most of all, you deserve to take a break once and for all from the exhausting hamster wheel of your mind, because you know there is another way. You can trust that it is all coming together without you mentally forcing everything into place, because your true self is orchestrating it. It is all you – and the you that worries is only a tiny fraction of all that you are.

The more you let go, the better it flows. You know this, because you have experienced it before. The more you trust, the more reasons you will be given to trust. The more you open to the divine in yourself, the more you will see the magic out there.

VISIONS FOR THE NEW EARTH

Every moment flows into the next in pure synchronicity, and we are marveling at the magic of it all. Everything we imagine, every intention we speak aloud, manifests into our reality with pure ease. It is almost as if it happens simultaneously – and it is hard to separate what comes first, the thought or the creation.

We are walking in a lucid dream, with childlike wonder, discovering a world of magic we never noticed before. It was always here, right in front of us, and yet somehow shielded from view. And now, it is undeniable.

We live in magic. We are magic.

Honoring Your Soul Signature

There will be seasons in your life for rest, enjoyment, and play. There will be other seasons when you will be inspired to pursue a vision, take action, and create something. But it will all feel the same to you, whether you are just enjoying your day or bringing a vision to life. It will all feel like you are just being yourself in every moment, following the highest joy and expression of who you are.

It will feel ecstatic to experience more of who you are, more of your infinite flavors, through the landscape of your life experiences. And this is because you are experiencing the same joy of creation as Source – experiencing all that you are and all that you can be.

From one perspective, each soul in a physical embodiment has a unique signature. This is your soul signature. It is your essence, the way you like to be and express who you are in this physical embodiment. Each soul is unique.

From another perspective, you are all one. And so, when you look at others and see their essence, you're seeing mirror reflections of yourself – experiencing more of yourself in other physical forms.

Both perspectives are true at the same time. But in this physical embodiment, you do have a unique essence that you have chosen to experience. You have gifts, things that come easily to you, preferences, and personality quirks… unique ways of seeing, being, and living that are your stamp on consciousness.

The variety of souls on Earth is magnificent because it allows you to experience all that you are, as well as the multifaceted variety of all that you can be, through seeing how others enjoy living and expressing who they are. It is the most beautiful world of mirrors. And because of this variety, you will create a New Earth bursting with creativity and color… each being following their joy, creating what they wish to create, holding the highest vision for the world they love.

Some will feel called to work with animals. Others will feel called to create new technologies, systems, and ways of working with energy and frequency. Many will be drawn to healing modalities, teaching and sharing wisdom, or creating events and offerings for the community. Others yet will love to make art or music, infusing beautiful frequencies into their creations. Others will design or build magical buildings and gathering spaces. And others will work with the land and plants.

And this is just the beginning. There are roles you cannot even fathom right now, as you collectively continue to expand upon life and all that is possible. As far as your imagination can stretch, the opportunities and ideas are endless. If you already love what you do now, it will continue to expand in magical ways, mirroring your expansion.

Some may have a focused passion and pursue that. That is beautiful. And others may have a multitude of interests, causes, and fields that they explore. That is beautiful too. But before you get bored with one thing, you will move on to something else. The New Earth is not linear. It is an ever-expanding multidimensional existence, mirroring the limitlessness and multifaceted nature of your being.

Practical Implementations

Does it sound too good to be true? You may wonder, if everyone is free to do whatever they want and no one has to work to survive, how the world will continue functioning. Who will drive the garbage trucks or work overtime at the hospitals?

This is a great question, but it's still being asked through the lens of the world that you know. The world you are entering is diametrically different in every way, shape, and form, including the availability of new technologies, tools, higher-frequency modalities, and inventions that seem light years ahead of their time. These will help make life so much easier and abundant for all.

Many of these inventions and tools already exist. Many of them were patented years ago, but your governments suppressed and banned them because they didn't want to lose their control and monopoly over major industries that would go bankrupt overnight if the new inventions were released to the world. For example, free energy was invented decades ago, but it has been discredited and suppressed because it threatens your entire oil and gas industry.

Even with the example of garbage disposal, humanity will discover technologies that can convert anything – waste, recyclables, even old clothes – into water or other useful materials. Everything is energy, and your new science will understand there are no limits to what can be done. This will completely revolutionize every facet of life.

The entire medical system will be transformed through the disclosure and release of highly advanced healing technologies that harness light and frequency for total body healing. While these technologies will be able to heal ailments and diseases, regrow limbs, restore your entire body to your pristine DNA blueprint, and more, the highest 'technology' will be the discovery of your own ability to self-heal through your super-consciousness. In time, disease will no longer exist, as humanity will be operating at a much higher frequency that will maintain the harmonious regeneration of the body.

There is no state of 'dis-ease' that can exist when your body is in harmony. On this ascension journey, you are unifying your body, mind, and soul to work in harmony. Your entire body is being upgraded in the image of the brilliant light that you are. You will no longer be a carbon-based human. Your body is becoming crystalline, vibrating at a much higher frequency. Your DNA is changing. You will no longer be the same species, and so the plagues (physical, mental, and emotional) that afflicted the carbon-based body will not apply.

This may seem far-fetched, but your DNA has already shifted immensely. You are not the same. The children being born now are not the same as the children born many generations ago. Their genetic coding is different. The amount of light they carry in their cells is different. Their connection to their heart and spirit is different.

Your entire relationship between self and community, and self and humanity, will change when you know that you are all one. Kindhearted people will rise to support those in need and rally to uphold and improve the functionality of their community. This will be fun, because there will be much more lightness, laughter, and play when people gather together and interact.

Right now, there may be certain roles that you see as below you, or service work that no one would like to do. But in a world where everyone is free to do whatever they wish, there will be plenty of people who feel fulfilled by serving in those ways, because it brings them joy to contribute to their community. This will bring them immense satisfaction in comparison to the life they were living before.

It's hard for the human to understand how all these changes will allow the world to continue to run, but trust that the world you are building will not have the limitations, lack, control, and suppression that you have experienced for centuries.

Money and other forms of exchange will continue to exist as long as your collective humanity decides they are needed. But your entire relationship with money will be upgraded. It will flow easily and be an abundant enabler of your dreams. Many who have more than enough will choose to circulate it and invest in the dreams of others. But in time, as you all remember you are creators, as you become the quantum field, the need for money as you know it will dissolve entirely. You will be able to create and magnetize to you everything that is needed. You will create new ways of exchanging and quantifying value for the purposes of clarity and communication with others.

When you know your power and the truth of how you create, you will receive the full experience of it. You will see how deliberately and precisely you can create. When all the noise of conflicting and limiting belief systems dissolves, you are left with the pure frequency of all that you are. And so, creation will become easier, faster, a clearer reflection of your truth. There will be no more resistance blocking that flow and connection. You will no longer have doubt, imposter syndrome, or insecurity. And this will feel incredibly liberating.

You can create any kind of world you desire. You can be anything you want. It will all come from a place of love, because your true essence is love. And so, you will create a life that you love, a world of love, a reality filled with love.

May your life be a reflection of your heart, the truth of your soul, the joy of being alive.

CHAPTER 12

A New Earth

This chapter is about where you are heading and what lies beyond, and it may require you to stretch your imagination beyond all limitation. Though you may have had glimpses of the energy of the New Earth emerging, you don't yet have proof, because it is still in the process of anchoring. So, the human part of you may feel hesitant to believe in the most beautiful version of Earth that can possibly exist, because what if it's too good to be true?

Your wildest dreams and the New Earth exist at a frequency beyond doubt. They materialize in a space where limitation and separation do not exist. And so, you will never trust in these visions if you try to analyze them with your mind, weighing up whether they're possible or not. It is more of a choice: which do you choose to feed, your doubts or your dreams? The old or the new? This is your reality, and you choose your experience.

The New Earth is not a faraway realm. It exists now. The heart of humanity has already spoken. You have already created the New Earth through the journey you have walked to get to this point. Your reality shifted with every moment that you sat with your emotions, alchemized the density, and stepped into your light. And the New Earth is birthed through your frequency, your open heart.

Individually, and collectively, you are calling forward the highest vision of the New Earth. It is a collective dream coming true.

Birthing the New Earth from Within

When you know yourself as the light, you'll know that this is the frequency of the New Earth. It is the same because when you anchor the frequency of all that you are and stand in your embodiment, it must be reflected back to you from your world. Your embodiment is what unlocks the New Earth. Holding its frequency within allows it to physically materialize before your eyes.

Most humans on this journey focus on what the New Earth looks and feels like as a physical experience, seeing it in separation. But in truth, it begins inside you. You will first notice it in the change in how you feel inside. The more you anchor the light, the more it anchors, so that it permanently materializes around you. You bring it to life in every moment that you choose to see it coming to life around you.

Anchoring the Light Activation:
Connecting with the New Earth

Go into nature and put your feet on the grass, connecting with the Earth. Imagine your energy flowing down into the Earth and the loving energy of the Earth flowing up into your heart. See everything around you with new eyes, as if you have never seen it before.

The New Earth is bursting forth in every corner of the world. The old is the echo of the past, and it is on its way out. Tune in to the higher frequencies that are already here.

I can feel this shift in my bones, because I experienced a day in Bali that felt similar to those 10 days that Joel and I had. It felt like a glimpse of the New Earth. And this time, it lasted about four or five exquisite hours.

At a tranquil café in Ubud, Bali, I joined a tea ceremony with five friends. I was the last to arrive at the low floor table, and there was already a grounded calmness amongst the group when we exchanged quiet hugs. In traditional ceremonial fashion, my friend prepared and poured ancient Chinese tea into our tiny ceramic cups. There was a meditative quality to slowly sipping the tea while we chatted about life.

It was a group of relatively new friends, two of whom I hadn't met before. This usually makes me feel a bit self-conscious, worried about what others may think of me or whether I'm contributing to the conversation. But I noticed myself breathing more slowly and deeply. The undercurrents of anxiety in my mind dissolved.

A blissful peace spread throughout my chest as I dropped into my heart. Instead of thinking about what to say next, I felt fully relaxed, without trying. There was no rush. No self-consciousness. No need to be anywhere or be anything.

Looking at me, my friend said, 'You seem so peaceful right now. So you. I haven't seen you like this in a long time.'

I was surprised, because I hadn't been 'doing' much. I was just sitting there, basking in the peace I felt in my heart, enjoying the company. I told him, 'I *feel* like me. I feel more like me right now than I have in a long time. My heart is open.'

He replied, 'It's beautiful to see you like this. You're shining brightly.'

It was so easy to be my true self. There was no thinking, simply a beingness melting into my heart. It felt like our entire group had entered another dimension, as we collectively held this higher frequency. Everyone looked shinier in a way, their eyes soft and relaxed. And I knew that this was the way to collectively shift; it was much easier to shift as an entire group when we held and embodied the higher frequencies together.

After a couple of hours, we hugged goodbye, and I flowed through the rest of my day with a smile in my heart. It was an ordinary day, but every moment felt different. I was in the frequency of divine connection with everything. Not wanting to check my phone, not needing to get anywhere or do anything in particular, I was simply happy to be.

I found myself smiling at the passersby and shopkeepers sitting on the steps outside their stores, and they smiled back. It was the same old concrete street with the cracked pavement, loud traffic, and taxi drivers sitting in the hot sun, calling out to solicit customers. But instead of seeing it through the eyes of lack or judgment, I saw the beauty of it all. I saw the soul of every being when I looked into their eyes. I saw the absolute perfection of it all. Maybe it had always been there, but I was seeing the world through brand-new eyes… as if I was a human experiencing life for the first time.

I realized I was hungry, so I went to a café down the street to have my favorite lunch. I ordered the Buddha bowl I'd had countless times, but it was as if I was tasting it for the first time, and the flavors exploded in my mouth with every bite. Absolutely delighted, I marveled at every mouthful.

When you embody the divine, you'll see the absolute perfection of everything through the eyes of God. You'll see the beauty of it all, including the density and remnants of the old. You won't have judgment anymore. The way you perceive your reality will change, and you'll lift the frequency of everything you see.

You'll know that wherever you go, whether you're in the most pristine setting in nature or in a loud city, it'll feel peaceful – because you'll be walking in pure presence and connection to yourself. This is how you bring the New Earth with you wherever you go, no matter what is happening around you.

As every being steps into this embodiment, of course you will gravitate toward breaking down what needs to be let go and creating improvements in the world. And so, the outer world will also shift in the way it looks and functions, but what will matter most to you is how you feel. It is the frequency that you embody that changes everything.

The Transition Period

Will there be an overnight shift? The answer is 'Yes and no.' The shift in frequency and dimension that you experience will be instant, tangible, and all-encompassing. It will be like those 10 days in a higher frequency that Joel and I experienced, but even more heightened and permanent.

How you feel inside will be powerfully buoyant, untouched by the old density – you will feel the divinity within you and all around you. This will change every experience, feeling, and interaction you have. You will know, without a doubt, that the world has changed.

At the same time, the world will go through a transition period, as it takes 'time' in your reality for the old systems and structures to be broken down and replaced by the new. You will witness the transition. At first glance, your reality may look the same as what you have known: same house, same roads, same trees. But when you look more closely, you'll notice a change in vibrancy – everything will be brighter and lighter, because of how you feel.

From where you are now, you may think it will take a long time for all the changes in the systems to take place on Earth. But know that many of these changes have already been happening in the background over decades. The foundation has been laid. There are key groups of visionaries, leaders, and lightworkers around the world who have been working on new solutions and systems, and these are ready to be implemented. Advanced technologies already exist, along with a fair economic system that is designed to help people to thrive, instead of perpetuating debt.

These systems aren't yet in the public eye and have been suppressed by governments and big corporations. But there will come a time when they will be revealed. There are already thousands of grassroots-led alternative communities in pockets around the world that are rejecting the current systems and choosing a new way of being.

Everything is unfolding in divine timing, in lockstep with the shifting consciousness of the people. Everything must happen at a pace that humanity can digest, because most will be utterly shocked when they awaken to the truths of the world and realize how much has been hidden from them.

The shifts are, however, already happening, and there will be a domino effect, with one setting off others. The ascension of humanity is speeding up exponentially, and millions and millions are awakening to the truths of their soul and the world. You have already passed the tipping point, and it cannot be slowed.

Those who have journeyed through the early waves of humanity's ascension – you who are reading this now – have anchored the higher frequencies so that more people can tune in to them. It becomes much easier for people to find that frequency within when they see others embodying their light.

Even those who aren't aware of the awakening are experiencing drastic changes. Their consciousness and bodies are shifting, along with the changing frequency of the collective and the Earth.

One day it will be as if a light switch has suddenly been turned on and the new systems, modalities, and technologies will be rolled out to the world. Those who spearhead these changes will be connected to their hearts and share them with transparency, for the good of the people. There will no longer be a concentration of power in the hands of the few at the top.

Some changes will be accepted very quickly, while others will take longer, but in time, people will rally behind them. Once people know how the systems and programming of the world have held them in a frequency of lack, fear, scarcity, and competition, they will no longer give their power away to them. So, the energies that kept you stuck in the loops of lower densities will be dissolved, along with the perceived pressures and limitations of life. You will realize that most humans are kind and loving, and just want to be able to enjoy life, love and be loved, and live freely without fear or lack.

> *Just wait and see how quickly you can change the world, when every being is free to live from the love in their heart.*

You may think it takes time to shift an entire world, but there are billions of you. All it takes is a small group to shift a community. All it takes is a few communities, coming together in harmony, to shift a world. All it takes is you, standing in your light. Those of you reading these words are pillars of light. When you come into wholeness within, the entire world shifts.

∞

As I write this, it has been four years since the magical 10 days that Joel and I had in a higher dimension. Where are we now?

Though Joel and I reminisce about those 10 days, we also feel like we have shifted immensely since then. Those 10 days felt like a gift, an experience of life in a higher dimension without any dips in frequency. But it felt like we were visiting that dimension as guests; it wasn't fully ours, as we hadn't yet embodied it in our cells.

Today, Joel and I are still growing on our ascension journey, and it's normal for us to wobble in frequency. We still dip into density and get stuck in our heads. We haven't yet experienced the same energy as those 10 days, sustained without wobbles over multiple days straight. At the same time, we feel constantly connected to that energy as it has anchored in us more and more. We feel remarkably more grounded in our light now than ever, even in those 10 days. This has been growing over time, but in the last six months we have jumped into new heights of trust and surrender in life, our inner guidance, and our path.

It feels more like an inner knowing – and even on days when we stray away from this, we can come back to our connection to the divine. Overall, we feel more stabilized in this frequency because we have anchored it; it cannot disappear or fade away, as it did at the end of those 10 days. Our hearts feel calm, and we are noticing more presence and surrender in our days.

Of course we have days when challenges come up or we feel thrown into the depths of density. But we do our best to allow ourselves to be with it, instead of judging or resisting it. We feel divinely supported with every step, even when we are struggling. No longer seeing this journey as a never-ending quest for self-improvement or a particular destination, we are enjoying life, surrendering to the journey, and showing up the best we can.

I'm realizing that this is the embodiment. This journey isn't just about feeling good and visiting a higher frequency... or about understanding these spiritual concepts intellectually. It's about knowing yourself and anchoring your light in your body, showing up in life as your embodied soul.

Often on this journey, it can feel like you are revisiting lessons or receiving the same reflections from your mirrorverse over and over again. You may think you already know these concepts and have mastered these lessons. But know that your journey is perfectly orchestrated to allow you to assimilate the higher energies from new vantage points – and in retrospect, you will see that you have always been expanding into your embodiment.

Joel and I know that the pace of this journey has been perfect for us, giving us the gift of fully participating in our ascension – feeling it all, facing our shadows, witnessing ourselves, and choosing our light over and over again. We are still in the process of clearing and integrating the most deeply rooted layers of density, the heaviest energies we have carried for lifetimes. And at times, this feels harder to face than anything we have had to endure thus far. But this is the place of deep alchemy, and we know we must go through it to know the wholeness of our light. We love where we are now, and the sense of peace in our hearts is everything. We value the frequency we are in now even more than that of those 10 days, because it truly feels like it is ours. We have anchored and embodied it, and it is expanding.

Trusting Your Path

There will come a time when you will feel the difference in your consciousness, physical body, and frequency. No longer trying to connect with your soul or inner knowing, you will live from that space.

You have asked yourself, over and over:

~ 'Is it true that I am connected to it all?'
~ 'Is it true that I create my reality?'
~ 'Is it true that I am ascending?'

But see how far you have come – from not even knowing about any of these concepts, to anchoring the light that you are, to the point where it is your lived reality.

You have been yearning to feel this way in your being. Just a few years ago, it would have felt like a miracle to feel this connected, in tune, and embodied. And because everything is shifting exponentially, just imagine what you will be experiencing one year from now.

The Earth will continue to go through its own process of purging, as people awaken to shocking truths and face everything they have been ignoring. Many will feel afraid and confused as the world they thought they knew turns upside down. But you have already gone through your awakening in your own timing – you have purged the majority of what you need to clear already. And so, you will be capable of holding the light while the rest of the world catches up. Your light will be a beacon of hope in their confusion, showing them that all is not lost.

There may come a time when others come to you, seeking answers and comfort, and you will know exactly what to say. And even when you feel like you're not doing enough, remember that you are on the leading edge of consciousness. Many around you are not even aware of 1 percent of what you have become aware of, what you have shifted within, and what you now know is possible.

You will feel untethered, unleashed, rising to the occasion because you know you came here for this time on Earth. You came here to be the light and help create the world to follow. And you are so ready.

When the time is right, you will be able to provide so much support to your friends, family, and community, simply by being yourself. For now, continue to trust your path and follow the nudges of your heart. Trust that you are doing more than enough, and it is all unfolding perfectly.

What Is the New Earth Like?

In a way, the New Earth is different for everyone, as each being holds their own vision for what is possible and what they want to experience in life. The New Earth is multidimensional and always expanding, so there is space for everyone's visions to materialize. What you experience and create will be what you choose, but as all will be living from their hearts and the truth of their souls, you'll find many similarities in your shared visions and values. Everyone will operate from a place of trust and limitlessness.

You'll be able to physically experience the New Earth just like you experience your current Earth. You'll walk upon it, smell it, touch it, and see it blooming before your eyes. It will be very real, and it will replace the world you have known. To you, it will feel as if the world you have known has suddenly shifted into a new vibration. From another perspective, the New Earth has always existed as a dimension overlaying your current world, just as all dimensions overlay each other. But you weren't able to perceive it until you tuned in to its frequency and anchored it from within.

> *The New Earth is not just a place or planet.*
> *It is your creation, a physical and energetic*
> *representation of the light you hold within.*

Just as all of your physical experiences are a mirror reflection of you, the New Earth is a reflection of you. And when the change you feel inside is mirrored to you by your physical world, you will no longer feel like you need to wait for your outer reality to catch up with the highest vision you hold within. It will be exactly the same as the vision you hold in your heart.

You will know the power of your imagination, because you will remember you created all of this with just your imagination. This world has told you imagination is child's play, when in truth it is the most powerful tool for creation in the universe. Your imagination is the key to creating anything. It is how you dream with no bounds, shatter all limitations, and birth new possibilities. The New Earth is a place to dream and imagine. You will unleash the full force of your imagination and creative power without any limits, without trying to control your visions with your mind.

Everything will lighten up, and nothing will be as serious as before. The density of the old world will feel like a faraway memory. You won't choose to tap into that frequency anymore, so you won't be able to replicate those old feelings of stress, worry, anxiety, or judgment. There will be nothing to prove, nothing to pull in or push away.

There will be a light-heartedness around you. You will know true play, joy, and laughter like never before. You have tasted it in your childhood, but you will experience the purest frequency of joy, with no density to counteract it. It will be joy without any twinge of bittersweetness or fear of losing that joy. In deep presence, you'll be able to give yourself fully to this energy and soak it in… without wondering if it's too good to be true or thinking about all the things you need to get done later. Adults have forgotten how to play, but in the New Earth, without the density in your being, it will feel easy to tap into the playfulness in you, because you will be both your inner child and highest self, embodied.

You will also experience a profound spiritual connection with all of life... nature, animals, people, the Earth, and yourself. You will be one with it all. You will experience a higher-frequency version of everything around you, because every atom and molecule will have shifted – from other people to the very air you breathe. All beings will finally know what it feels like to live in unconditional love... and you will walk in full reverence that the spirit in you is the same as the spirit in everything else.

This births a world overflowing with beautiful communities, loving interactions between people, and creations from the heart that benefit all. You will experience more harmony and love with your family and friends, entire communities, and humanity as a whole.

You will know that the Earth is an aspect of yourself. You will develop a friendship with it, creating in harmony with the land, receiving and giving with pure gratitude as you build thriving ecosystems that support all.

As you activate the full expression of your DNA, higher mind, and cellular structure, you will be able to perceive more vibrancy and intricacy in colors. You will see everything much more clearly, and this will also be because you will drop into new depths of presence beyond anything you have ever experienced.

Simply being present and looking at the world, you will be enchanted as you feel utter peace flowing through your body. There will be no tension, resistance, or fear. You will never be bored, because simply breathing will feel scrumptious.

There will be no rush to be anywhere but where you are, knowing every moment is sacred and exactly where you're meant to be. You will feel giddy, in love with life, appreciating everything within you and around you, without trying.

You will be able to be all that you are and do whatever you want, so every day will feel absolutely freeing and weightless. At the same time, you'll feel innately connected to your heart, overflowing with inspiration and excitement for all that you wish to create. Everything you wish to create will flow with ease. Creation will feel as easy as breathing, because this is who you are.

VISIONS FOR THE NEW EARTH

You will tell the story of your ascension for years to come, because it will be the story of your life, looking back.

You will say, 'This was the time our entire world turned upside down. And this was how we found our way back to our hearts. This synchronicity led to this moment, then this epiphany. This was how we came together as humanity.'

You will tell your story to your friends, when they awaken in their own time. You will tell strangers in the street, because they will listen and tell you theirs, too. You will tell your children and grandchildren, until they know it by heart.

And it will be the most common story ever told... a story that never gets old. This is the biggest event humanity has ever experienced, and this is why it will ultimately unite humanity like never before.

It will bring people together who thought they had nothing at all in common, because they will know that at their core, they are the same. Their stories will be different, but their hearts will be one.

You are living this story now.

You are creating it as you go.

And so, you might as well make it good.

At the end of it, you will see that you are not divided. You are one.

Your story is the story of humanity – the most incredible tale of love and triumph.

Just wait until you see the entire multiverse hold its breath, in awe of you, honoring you… hanging on to your every word.

Onward

You came here not only for this ascension, but for what is next. This ascension is just the beginning.

You exist, and you create. This is a natural part of who you are. You are expanding infinitely, while at the same time, fully being here now. This is the dance between existing in pure presence and creating, with both happening simultaneously.

In forgetting and remembering who you are, you get to awaken to the brilliance of life and your own soul. You get to see the beauty of who you are as Source, experiencing it as if for the first time, even though it is who you have been for eternity. And you get to express yourself as the individual you are in this lifetime, sending an echo into the fabric of consciousness that ripples out across all the dimensions of existence.

What do you create from this embodiment? Who do you choose to be? How do you feel, as you experience all that you are?

Of course, you have done this over and over again, infinite times, in infinite ways. You have come back to this moment to experience it now. At the same time, you are creating yourself for the first time. It sounds contradictory, but it is true.

And here you are. All of creation is so excited to see what happens at this edge of consciousness. What kind of world will humanity create, when everyone begins to live from the remembrance of who they truly are?

The veil will drop from your eyes. You will see the truth of who you are, of this reality, of your infinite potential... the immense magic, power, and love in your being. What you create will be beyond your wildest dreams, beyond anything you can imagine now, with more love in your heart than you have ever felt.

You will stop living from the vantage point of just this one incarnation and identity that you believe yourself to be... and begin living as the infinite consciousness that you are.

You will create your next ascension, and the next. There has been so much focus on this ascension, but in truth you are continuously ascending and expanding into all that you are and all that you can be. Source is constantly expanding, and so you are constantly expanding. As you ascend, you will continue dreaming and stretching your imagination to new heights.

There may come a time when you feel your experience on the New Earth is complete and you're ready for what's next. You may choose to explore other dimensions and realms, and you can, because they're all within you. Using your frequency, imagination, and ability to feel all the potentialities, you will be able to attune yourself to any dimension you want to experience.

You will see and experience energy as it is, without the illusion of time or separation of space. And this is how you can shift your consciousness to any existence, reality, and timeline. You will want to experience yourself in infinite ways, because this is who you are.

Anything you can imagine already exists, and you get to choose what you pull into your reality and how you experience it. You will be able to tap into other dimensions in your dream state and meditations, and perceive other realms while standing exactly where you are. In addition, you will be able to take your body with you and physically materialize into other dimensions. And whenever you want, you can also choose to 'return' to Source, simply being in that Oneness and bliss.

There may also be a point when you consciously choose to leave your body, knowing that it's not a death but a transition. It is also possible for your body's frequency to vibrate at such a high rate that it becomes pure light, and you can take it with you into the highest dimensions, where everything is light.

You may choose to go back to Earth and forget who you are again, or go to another planet or plane of existence that's similar to Earth. You may choose to ascend into completely unrecognizable realities.

You may choose to experience all of this and more at once. What's available to you is infinitely vaster and more majestic than you can fathom from your current point of consciousness. Your ascension in this lifetime is just the beginning of ever-expanding ascensions.

Here is one way to visualize the infinite nature of consciousness. Imagine the multiverse is one droplet of water in the ocean. This droplet holds the totality of everything that you know and can possibly imagine: the Earth, nature, humanity, the dimensions, the sun, and concepts like universes, timelines, and parallel realities. Everything that you can possibly conceive of exists in this one droplet. But this is only one droplet among infinite droplets, expanding infinitely in all directions.

Imagine each droplet is a multiverse of its own. There is no way to describe or comprehend what the other multiverses are like, because if you can describe or comprehend something, it exists in your multiverse.

What you can say is that the other multiverses do not look like how you picture yours. They do not operate according to the same natural laws; many do not even have similar concepts of worlds, dimensions, time, space, or matter, though others will have similarities to your multiverse. Some multiverses may appear more energetic and others more physical, at varying degrees of complexity. This is still, however, an inadequate attempt at applying words to something that cannot be described.

From this perspective, it can feel like you are minuscule. But at the same time, you are not just this droplet, you are all of them. This droplet is only a tiny fractal of all that you are: God, experiencing itself infinitely. And so, the only thing that connects these droplets as one infinite ocean of consciousness is God. God is infinite. Even the most infinite idea of God that you can imagine is just the beginning of God.

But then, does it even matter what happens in your multiverse droplet? Nothing matters, and at the same time, everything matters. Everything matters, because everything is sacred. Everything is a piece of the whole.

It's not what you do that matters, it's who you are and who you know yourself to be. You chose to have these experiences to know yourself infinitely and to keep expanding upon the creation of all that is. This is your greatest joy.

Your ascension in this life into knowing yourself as God matters because it affects all timelines and dimensions, lifting the consciousness of your entire multiverse. And this sets off a chain reaction that ripples out to all the other multiverses. Your ascension sparks a wave of light spreading across the infinite ocean of all that is.

Many multiverses have life-forms, though they are completely unlike how you may view life. But not every multiverse explores the concept of life that can become conscious of itself. Everything is God, everything is consciousness, but not all of consciousness has the capacity to become aware of itself or ascend into knowing itself as God. And so, what you are achieving in your multiverse is a magnificent feat. Even the concept of ascension as you know it is unique to your multiverse, though other multiverses may explore similar journeys in their own ways.

The journey you're taking in this life, from descending into forgetting all that you are to remembering again, is monumental, even in the ocean of infinite multiverses. As a metaphor, at this moment your multiverse droplet is glowing brightly, sparkling amongst the other multiverses swirling in the ocean of consciousness. And that light is spreading to illuminate all those around it.

∞

Your soul yearns to know yourself even beyond this multiverse. What lies beyond this multiverse? You already know that you will find more of yourself – more of God. But what does that look or feel like?

There may come a point where you choose to explore that. As you ascend, your vibrational frequency speeds up. This allows you to perceive and anchor more of who you are, expanding your consciousness to embody more of who you have always truly been.

This expansion of your consciousness may even birth entirely new multiverses. You are limitless, reality is malleable, and the infinite ocean of existence shifts in response to you.

What will you choose?

∞

You are the one writing this book. It is a message from another aspect of your soul to you. A communication between you and you. This is the cosmic dance of you, you, and more of you.

Everything you have ever experienced has been a gift from your soul to awaken you to more of who you are… to help you choose who you want to become… and to show you how your frequency creates what's next.

The boundary between you and your outer reality is dissolving. You are seeing how your frequency affects your reality, and how quickly your reality responds to you. It is not even responding to you – it *is* you. The inner reality becomes the outer reality. There is no distinction.

You will know that all of it is your consciousness when you feel your soul stretching everywhere… when your body becomes the galaxies and your heart beats with every twinkle of the stars above… when your feet become the Earth, and your breath becomes the whispers of the wind… when your consciousness can see it all and hold it all.

You will know it has always been you.

*May all beings
come home to their light.*

Thank You

Thank you from the bottom of my heart to everyone who helped bring this book to life, and especially to those whose light has forever touched my soul.

To my husband, Joel Munyard – you are the spectacular love, companion, and mirror of my life. Every day, I'm in awe that we get to journey this deeply together as we expand into knowing all that we are. You have shown me the infinite capacity of love, and our soul connection is the greatest gift of my life.

To my parents, Vivek and Kumiko Pathela – you have always encouraged me to reach for the stars and follow my artistic heart. As I walk into motherhood, I have an even greater appreciation for all that you are, and all that you have been to me. I am beyond blessed that you are my parents.

To my sister, Maya Pathela – you have shown me the beauty of keeping your heart soft in a hardened world. You are a pure light on this Earth.

To my incredible editor, Lizzie Henry; the team at Hay House – Amy Kiberd, Grace Rahman, Leanne Siu Anastasi, and the extended team; and to the wider Penguin Random House family. It felt like we were destined to bring this book to life together. Thank you for your unwavering dedication and, most of all, for honoring my heart's voice every step of the way. Amy, your belief in me from the very beginning made all the difference – thank you.

To Bonnie Karuna Smith, my dear friend and the artist behind this book's cover painting – I had a specific vision for the energy of this book, and it would not be *Anchoring the Light* without your stunning artwork. Thank you for channeling this energy into every brushstroke, so that people all over the world can feel this book in their hearts before they even read a word. You are a radiant light in my life.

To my extended family and soul sisters who have always been there for me, loving me for who I am, reminding me of my light when I forget – you know who you are. I cherish each of you.

To Melissa Hadfield and Crystal Allen ('The Energetic Alchemist') – you are brilliant beacons of light on this ascension path, and your soul guidance has inspired me more than you can know. Thank you for your friendship, for holding the vision steady and showing the way.

To my beloved son, Elokai Ari Munyard, and future child(ren) – thank you for choosing me to be your mama. You are my miracles, my heart's greatest expansion, my life's joy. I love you and your dad beyond this realm, beyond anything I have known.

To Bodhi – I love you forever. You were the greatest pup, my heart's purest companion. Our family. I miss you with everything, but I feel you everywhere.

To my online community – thank you for journeying alongside me, showing me that I'm not alone or crazy! You are my soul family.

And to you, dear reader – thank you for opening your heart to these words. If this book has touched your heart, it is because it reflects a knowing deep within. Thank you for shining your unique light on this Earth.

With love,
Ashmi

About the Author

Ashmi Pathela is a writer, artist, and visionary guide for this unprecedented time of global ascension. Her words, courses, ceremonies, and workshops have touched the lives of hundreds of thousands of people all over the world.

In 2017, she left a thriving career in Silicon Valley to follow her heart. Today, she guides others on the journey of embodying the light of their soul through her writing and online offerings.

Ashmi now lives in Denmark, Western Australia, where she and her husband are creating a healing sanctuary and retreat center.

For soul guidance and multidimensional channelings, follow Ashmi on Instagram: **@ashmi.path**

Explore her books, courses, online ceremonies, and activations here: **www.ashmipathela.com**

TRANSFORM YOUR DAY— ANYTIME, ANYWHERE

With the **Empower You** Unlimited Audio *App*

❝ ★★★★★ **Life changing.**
My fav app on my entire phone, hands down! – Gigi ❞

Unlimited access to the entire Hay House audio library!

You'll get:

- 600+ soul-stirring **audiobooks** to expand your mind
- 1,000+ **meditations** for restful sleep, morning focus, and gentle healing
- Bite-sized audios **under 20 minutes**—perfect for busy days
- **Exclusive talks** you won't find anywhere else
- **Daily affirmations**
- Fresh content added **every week** to fuel your journey

Listen to the audio version of this book!

❝ Driving, yard work, and housework have been **transformed**! – Ruffles27 ❞

Scan the QR code to start listening or visit **hayhouse.com/unlimited**

We hope you enjoyed this Hay House book. If you'd like to receive our online catalogue featuring additional information on Hay House books and products, please contact:

Hay House UK Ltd
1st Floor, Crawford Corner,
91–93 Baker Street, London W1U 6QQ
Tel: +44 (0)20 3927 7290; www.hayhouse.co.uk

Published in the United States of America by:
Hay House LLC
PO Box 5100, Carlsbad, CA 92018-5100
Tel: (760) 431-7695 or (800) 654-5126
www.hayhouse.com

Published in Australia by:
Hay House Australia Publishing Pty Ltd
18/36 Ralph St., Alexandria NSW 2015
Tel: +61 (02) 9669 4299
www.hayhouse.com.au

Published in India by:
Hay House Publishers (India) Pvt Ltd
Muskaan Complex, Plot No. 3,
B-2, Vasant Kunj, New Delhi 110 070
Tel: +91 11 41761620
www.hayhouse.co.in

Let Your Soul Grow

Experience life-changing transformation – one video at a time – with guidance from the world's leading experts.

www.healyourlifeplus.com

CONNECT WITH
HAY HOUSE
ONLINE

hayhouse.co.uk   @hayhouse

@hayhouseuk   @hayhouseuk.bsky.social

@hayhouseuk   @HayHousePresents

Find out all about our latest books & card decks • Be the first to know about exclusive discounts • Interact with our authors in live broadcasts • Celebrate the cycle of the seasons with us • Watch free videos from your favourite authors • Connect with like-minded souls

'The gateways to wisdom and knowledge are always open.'

Louise Hay